MW01094804

INCREASE OF THE KINGDOM

Tudor Bismark

INCREASE
~ of the ~
KINGDOM

TUDOR BISMARK

Increase of the Kingdom
By Tudor Bismark
© 2014 by Tudor Bismark Ministries

ISBN: 978-0-9841940-3-2

Content Development by Sozo Publishing Group
Published by Sozo Publishing Group, sozopublishing.com

Printed in the United States of America by Tudor Bismark Ministries

We dedicate this book to the Late Honorable Dr. Myles Munroe and Ruth, his wife and the Love of his life.

We had the wonderful and distinct privilege to minister with and share in the unique life of Dr. Myles and Ruth.

I had a brother RELATIONSHIP with Dr. Myles, myself being the younger brother. I learned so much for so long from him. His revelation knowledge on "The Kingdom" further embellished our teachings and our culture of "The Kingdom." I cannot express enough in words how much that influenced our ministry and my own life.

Few in history in "The Body of Christ" have made such significant contributions in political, economic, social and religious circles as Dr. Munroe. It will take years for anyone to rise up and achieve the same levels of influence in these respective sectors as he has.

Dr. Munroe is/was a TRUE example and penultimate ambassador of "The Kingdom," and for this we are eternally grateful.

Our prayer is for his son, Myles Jr., and daughter, Charisa, to be successful in all they do and to be blessed immensely.

Bishop Tudor Bismark

CONTENTS

INCREASE OF THE KINGDOM

INTRODUCTION

Increase of the Kingdom is a continuation of our messages and books on the Kingdom. Our first book released in the previous decade was *The Kingdom in Motion*, followed by The *Order of the Kingdom*. In ten years, the urgency of this message has only increased in my spirit, as I believe it becomes more and more timely with each passing year. I feel strongly about the message of the Kingdom; it is not a message about religion, but rather a message regarding experience that will eventually become a lifestyle or culture, shaping the world around us. Jesus taught about the Kingdom more than any other subject.

In this book, I will rely on three foundational scriptures, beginning with Isaiah 9:6: "For unto us a child is born, unto us a son is given: and the government shall be upon his shoulder: and his name shall be called Wonderful, Counsellor, the mighty God, the everlasting Father, the Prince of Peace." The second foundational text is found in Matthew 6:33: "But seek ye first the kingdom of God, and his righteousness; and all these things shall be added unto you." The third verse is found in the last book of the Bible, Revelation 20:1, and is the "anchor" throughout the book: "And I saw an angel come down from heaven, having the key of the bottomless pit and a great chain in his hand." As is customary in my books, there will be many Biblical references throughout, but these three will serve as the foundation for this particular Kingdom message.

Isaiah is probably the most well-known of the Old Testament prophets, as well as the most significant. Much of his writing throughout the sixty-six chapters of his book pertains to the Messiah. Isaiah is filled with Messianic references—His message as well as His destiny and purpose. Chapters 1–39 reflect the temperament of the Old Testament, but the final 27 chapters, 40–66, are congruous with the New Testament books from Matthew through Revelation and are extremely relevant to the message of the Kingdom.

In Chapter 66 of the book of Isaiah, the prophet spoke of a nation being born in one day. Though interpretations abound, I believe this verse means that the Kingdom of God will be implemented in a specific season. Isaiah 9:6 tells us, "For unto us a Child is born and unto us a Son is given. And the government will be upon His shoulder." Children are born and sons are given, and we cannot establish the Kingdom of God without government. The ruling government is the administration that establishes the laws and is given the power to legislate what happens in the country. Verse 6 of Isaiah 9 continues, "And His Name shall be called Wonderful, Counselor, the Mighty God, the Everlasting Father, the Prince of Peace."

This book, *Increase of the Kingdom*, is based on the very next Scripture, Isaiah 9:7: "Of the increase of His government and peace, there shall be no end. Upon the throne of David and over his kingdom, to order it and establish it with judgment and with justice from henceforth even forever. The zeal, the zeal of the Lord will perform this." We see here a significant prophecy regarding the increase of His government and peace; there will be no end to it, and upon the throne of David and upon his kingdom, ordered and established with judgment and justice even forever. As the first coming of Jesus was prophesied, and it did happen, then we must also believe that the second part of this prophesy has come, will come and is coming. This is the point of our focus: The Kingdom of God within the earth is going to be significant.

As we begin to work with the Book of Revelation, I want to deal with a viewpoint which is eschatological in nature. Eschatology is the teaching of the last days and the return of Jesus. There are many schools of thought regarding the last days. One belief is that Jesus will rapture (catch away) the church, and, following the rapture of the church on earth, there will be a demonic reign of terror. Traditionally this belief has three divisions classified as: pre-tribulation (the church will be raptured before the Great Tribulation begins); mid-tribulation (the church will be taken before the most heinous of judgments are released); or post-tribulation (the church will endure the Great Tribulation). The Great Tribulation has been known as a period of seven years in which the wrath of God will be poured out upon the earth. Following the tribulation, Jesus will return with His Church and will set up a thousand years of peace on the earth, known as The Millennium, while at the same time, satan will be cast into the bottomless pit.

Another school of thought, which I tend to lean toward, is based upon a different Biblical worldview. This school of thought asserts that a generation will emerge upon the earth which will become so ingrained with Kingdom principles, with Kingdom behavior and Kingdom lifestyle that they will release in the earth the dynamics of the Kingdom of God and literally displace the power of the devil. He will then be replaced so powerfully that the culture of the enemy and the demonic, luciferian dogma will be powerless in the earth for a thousand years. It is from this viewpoint that I want to discuss Revelation 20.

John, the Revelator, said, "And I saw an angel come down from heaven, having the key of the bottomless pit and a great chain in his hand." The word "angel" is "messenger" or, in this instance, "apostolic messenger." The Bible says in Matthew 16:13–19, "Peter said, 'Thou art the Christ the Son of the living God,' and Jesus said, 'Flesh and blood hath not revealed this to you but my Father which is in Heaven.' " Peter, as the "apostolic messenger" was given the keys to the Kingdom of Heaven. Whatever he loosed on earth was loosed; whatever he bound on earth was bound. So Peter bound some things in the earth with the keys he was given.

Now we understand, "…an angel came down from heaven…" who was an apostolic messenger with the keys to bind things. He held the keys to the bottomless pit as well as a great chain in his hand. The chain here is the three-fold cord. The Bible says in 1 Corinthians 13:13, "now abideth faith, hope, and charity…"—the three-fold cord chain—the power of faith, the power of hope, and the power of love. He's holding this in his hand; and he's going to chain this devil, bind him, and remove the culture in the earth. Now watch—the generation emerges "and laid hold of the dragon, the old serpent, the devil and satan, and bound him for a thousand years." The word "bind" here is not necessarily "tie" as when the apostle was told, "What you bind on earth will be bound in heaven…." This indicates that what comes out of the culture out of the prophetic mouth of believers actually binds a demonic system.

From the time satan deceived Eve to the time that Jesus came and bruised the head of satan, a period of 4000 years, satan ruled the earth. But as the believing generation arises, this demonic system is bound and cast into the bottomless pit. This doesn't necessarily mean hell. Anything that's bottomless means it has no foundation. So, satanic dogma has no foundation—he's bound and cast into a system that has no foundation. He is cast into a system that keeps spiraling and going downward because it has no foundation.

Why? We are built upon the foundation of the apostles and the prophets. A generation will emerge that's built on the foundation of apostles and prophets; and once it does, the church will be established in a very significant way. The generation of the Kingdom people who are on the earth will be so convinced, so empowered with Kingdom principles that its behavior, its lifestyle, and its culture will literally replace demonic culture.

When Jesus came, He gave power to His church, saying, "Upon this rock, I will build my church." For the last 2000 years, the church has been established in the earth. Now, please realize there's a difference between the Church and the Kingdom. The Church is the legal and legitimate tool through which the Kingdom of God is established. Jesus preached the Kingdom; Paul preached the Kingdom; and all the apostles of God preached the Kingdom. It is clear in Matthew 24:14,

"This gospel of the Kingdom shall be preached in all the earth; then shall the end come." Until the gospel of the Kingdom is preached, the end is not coming.

A generation will emerge that will not only preach the gospel of the Kingdom but also they will live it, testify and spread it. And when that generation comes, everything we see of satanic influence, satanic behavior, everything we see as satanic, and every demonic stronghold will be displaced and will be cast into systems that have no foundations—the bottomless pit. Verse 3 says "You will cast him into the bottomless pit and shut it and seal him where he will deceive the nations no more for a thousand years." The capability to "seal him" is by the power of the Holy Spirit. The Bible tells us in Ephesians 1:13, "In Him you also trusted...having believed, you were sealed with the Holy Spirit of promise." It is the earnest or first fruits of our inheritance. This seal of the Holy Spirit, which is going to be the empowerment structure for believers, is going to keep the devil bound for one thousand years.

Most believers who are reading this book have prayed prayers of binding the devil and loosing things in the earth; however, the best way to make that happen is to begin to live the life of the believer. There are three ways in which we move the devil:

1. We rebuke him. We speak it.
2. We displace him. We bring apostolic and prophetic rank into a place or atmosphere to move him out.
3. We replace him. We receive systematic teaching where a seed is sown which grows into an experience. Mark 4:29–32 relates that the seed of the experience of God goes throughout the earth:

> *But when the grain is ripe, at once he puts in the*
> *sickle, because the harvest has come." And he*
> *said, "With what can we compare the kingdom of God,*
> *or what parable shall we use for it? It is like a grain of*
> *mustard seed, which, when sown on the ground, is the*

smallest of all the seeds on earth, yet when it is sown
it grows up and becomes larger than all the garden
plants and puts out large branches, so that the birds of
the air can make nests in its shade. (ESV)

Our responsibility is not only to displace the devil but also to replace him. We must remove him completely by bringing the Kingdom of God into full manifestation.

First Corinthians 12 states we are all members of one body, and Christ is the head. The head is in place, but we as the body have not yet been the significant force He could work through. Ezekiel 37 describes the valley of dry bones which depicts a place of worldliness. The members of the body begin coming together as the prophetic word is released. Once this happens, the headship of Christ shall bring the increase of His government which shall have no end. The government is going to be on the shoulders of his body, the church, and it will displace the force of the enemy.

Following are ten points concerning the way the Kingdom of God functions:

1. The nature of the Kingdom is increase.
2. The dynamic of the Kingdom is that everything gets better.
3. The power of the Kingdom is force.
4. The culture of the Kingdom is service.
5. The order of the Kingdom is structure.
6. The anointing of the Kingdom is gifts.
7. The success of the Kingdom is generational dominion.
8. The currency of the Kingdom is faith.
9. The strength of the Kingdom is unity.
10. The access to the Kingdom is in understanding mysteries.

Through the course of this book, each of these ten thoughts and ideas will be developed. Understand that the foundational truth these ten points rest upon is found in Luke 17. Luke 17:20 states, "And when He was demanded of the Pharisees when the Kingdom of God should come, He answered them and said, 'The Kingdom of God does not come with observation; neither shall they say, go here or go there, for behold the Kingdom of God is within you.'" The Kingdom of God does not come with observation, but rather it is within us and must be activated.

One of my favorite pastimes, especially when traveling, is to sit in airports and watch people. I was in Abidjan recently; and each morning, I would go out early in the morning to sit in the foyer of my hotel and just watch people. Now there are various peoples in the region who have been separated geographically by demarcations of the French and British. There are people from the same cultures or tribal groups who were separated several centuries ago; yet they retain similar behavior and mannerisms. The languages, however, in different regions are influenced by the culture.

As I observe them in the airport, it is easy to assume which country each person is from, but until I actually interact with them, I cannot know their country of origin for certain. I cannot determine their tribe or ethnicity simply by observation.

Jesus said the Kingdom of God is the same way—it does not come by observation, but by demonstration. We have been given the tools to activate the culture of God in the earth. When Jesus said "the Kingdom of God is within you," He meant that the potential for the culture of God to dominate the earth is within every one of us. Within us is the potential to be successful, the potential to be prosperous, and the potential to bring elevation in the earth; and that potential was placed there by God. Understand, however, and remember: It does not come by observation; it comes when we activate the Kingdom of God within ourselves.

Increase is in us because the Kingdom of God is within us. Structure, order, and power are within us because the Kingdom of God is in us. Let's look at the Kingdom message beginning with Adam who came into the earth as the son of God. If God is the King of the universe, what would you call the son? You call him a prince, Prince Adam. When a prince comes into a kingdom domain through birth, it means that at some point, the prince has the potential to become the king.

It's unusual for a prince to be a king when his father is still alive. One of three things has to happen for that to occur:

1. The father has to die to make the prince the ruling monarch.
2. The king, the father, has to abdicate his throne and give it to his prince.
3. The father has to allow his son to create another kingdom, and they both reign as kings over their individual kingdoms.

God is King of the whole earth. He is King of the universe. When God birthed His son, Adam, in the earth, He gave dominion over the earth to Adam. He created the Kingdom of God on earth and gave Adam kingdom rights. All of the offspring of Adam since that time are princes and princesses. We are children of a Kingdom order. When Adam sinned against God, his kingdom was taken over by a demonic system.

According to Matthew 12, the demonic system is a kingdom of its own. In Matthew 12:25–50, Jesus said, "Every kingdom divided against itself cannot stand. And if satan be divided against satan, how then shall his kingdom stand?" Satan's kingdom is standing; and he is the king in his kingdom. He became a king by deceiving Eve in the garden and usurping Adam's authority, and thus Adam became a slave in the devil's kingdom. As a slave, you must pay tribute to the kingdom in which you belong, even if it formerly belonged to you.

For this reason, Adam and his children became slaves to the satanic kingdom, and we have been paying tribute ever since. When Jesus came, He came to restore His kingdom. In John 18:33, Pilate asked Jesus, "Are You the King…?" Jesus answered, "My kingdom is not of this world…." In other words, Jesus made it known that he was not part of the Roman system, but of the heavenly system. Jesus is King of His Kingdom.

After Jesus died, and the Day of Pentecost birthed the Church, the monarchy was reestablished. Everyone that now becomes born again into the Kingdom through the Spirit is a prince or princess, ruling and reigning with Him in heavenly places. Matthew 4:17 tells us the Kingdom of heaven has arrived and has been established within the earth. Jesus preached the kingdom throughout the gospels with Acts 1:1–7 being the final thought—"To you, Theophilus, I've come to tell all the things that Jesus began both to do and to teach. How that after His resurrection, Jesus appeared to His disciples forty days and nights speaking to them in many infallible truths concerning the kingdom of God." And He told them to go to Jerusalem and wait until they received power from on high. The disciples asked Him, "Will You restore the kingdom to Israel at this time?" He replied, "It's not for you to know the times and the seasons that the Father has placed in His own hands." In other words, the kingdom is going to be restored in its time; you go to Jerusalem and wait to be activated in the power of the Holy Spirit.

Jesus began His ministry preaching the Kingdom which lasted until He was about to leave the earth. The last thing He spoke to His disciples was continued teaching on the infallible truths of the Kingdom. Let me give you this scenario: If I were leaving for a trip, I might ask a friend to come housesit for me. As Pastor ChiChi and I walk out the door, we'd give him instructions on caring for our pets, our cars and our home. Those would be the important tasks at hand that would need attention immediately. They are not details or directions for the months out in the future; they are the immediate instructions. Before Jesus left, His immediate concerns were to hand over His responsibilities to His followers, so what did He do? He continued teaching what He had always taught—the Kingdom message.

In Acts 28:30–31, the Bible says, "And Paul was in his own hired house for two years, receiving such to see him, and there he spent time, preaching Christ and teaching the Kingdom. That's all Paul did. He preached the Kingdom.

What is the Kingdom? It's a lifestyle; it's a culture; it's a spirit of dominion. It is a spirit that displaces demonic influence. The Kingdom removes satanic dogma, thinking and culture from our society—so much so, that satan has no room. For this to happen in our lives, we must make sure that we are empowered with the Kingdom message. We must fully understand that the Kingdom of God must be activated.

So the Bible tells us this: Jesus preached the Kingdom; Paul preached the Kingdom; and the apostles preached the Kingdom. Matthew 10:7 says, "Go you to the lost house of Israel and as you go, preach, saying, 'The Kingdom of God is at hand'." For generations, the apostles preached the Kingdom message until the 3rd and 4th centuries A.D. when the Roman culture began to spread.

The word "apostle" is not a religious word; it's not a church word. It's actually a Roman word that's used in warfare meaning "forerunner". An apostle would go in front of an army to spy out the area and set up a strategic base for the army that was coming. Then they would send word back and say, "We are now ready to receive the invading forces." Caesar was the first apostle in that era.

This apostle, Caesar, and his men were struggling with this new group that had no weapons and were following Jesus; they were empowered by love; and they were taking over everywhere. Their doctrine taught that there was a King, but the Romans couldn't find this king because He had risen from the dead and ascended to heaven. They tried to find this King and began to arrest and torture Christians. They would beat them and say, "We know you're hiding your King! Where is He?" Caesar knew that, as long as their King was alive, these people would be empowered. He believed that, if he could kill the King, the whole movement would scatter.

For three hundred years, they couldn't find this King. Finally, it dawned upon those in Rome that this King they were talking about was some fictitious being in the heavens. At this point, Caesar himself decided he would join this group and become a Christian. When he did, he brought Roman culture and Jewish culture together with Christian culture and joined all of their symbols, including religious symbols and rituals. This made the whole thing legal under one universal church. This decision disenfranchised the message of the Kingdom.

When that happened, the power of the Kingdom was grossly impaired and broken. Instead of moving from apostolic and prophetic headship, religious leaders were appointed by the state. They were men that were not apostolic, but were appointed because they had favor—favor with Caesar and favor with the system.

When that church and system began, the message of the Kingdom became diluted until it was rarely preached. Access to the Bible became less and less. Fewer people knew the Scriptures. The Church at that time moved from being among the people into centers. The first church building was built in the 4th Century A.D.; and people no longer met in the marketplace or moved house-to-house sharing the message of the Kingdom. Instead, they met in a building, where church became a weekly experience, led by an appointed individual who talked in a language that the people didn't understand. The Kingdom message was weakened, and deception crept into the church. Many satanic behaviors and symbols began to emerge within the body of Christ; and this continued for many, many centuries.

However, in more recent years, there has been a revival of the kingdom message, not as a denomination, but as a behavior. The Kingdom of God must be preached in all the earth. It's God's nature in the earth. It's God's nature here among us; so it is important that we understand that the Kingdom of God has come to be set up in the earth. The devil destroyed the kingdom message by introducing and emphasizing his own message. Now it is time to restore the message of the kingdom to the body of Christ and to the world.

A number of people have expressed concern that evil is so rampant in the earth that it will eventually take over. People think the nations will never turn away from idolatry. Drug addiction, sexual pornography, murder, religious persecution, growing anxiety, and discontent abound; indeed, it appears that we are not moving toward righteousness, but rather toward evil and destruction. However, do not be misled by what you see. Imagine that God's Kingdom is like a computer. If a virus invades the computer, it is taken to a technician for repair. Perhaps he will simply load anti-virus software and remedy the problem. Or perhaps he will wipe the hard drive and begin again. Regardless, the technician will identify the problem, repair it, and restore the computer to be fully functional. Likewise, a generation of people will emerge with the Kingdom message indelibly printed on their hearts and streaming from their lips; and it will eradicate the cancerous sin virus intruding into God's Kingdom. The Kingdom Generation will abolish the lies and deception of the enemy with the razor sharp truth of the Kingdom message. The family of man will be restored; and it will happen quickly. Simultaneously, we will experience a massive visitation from God; He will literally "pour out His Spirit on all flesh." When this real authentic move of God comes, it will be a fulfilment of Habakkuk 2:14 saying, "For the earth will be filled with the knowledge of the glory of the Lord as the waters cover the sea."

How will this generation emerge? In every human being there is a brain; within every brain there is a mind. Within every mind there is a belief system or a culture. Within every belief system there is a shaper. And with every shaper, there is an agenda. Every belief system has a shaper and every shaper has an agenda.

Romans 10:17 tells us that, "Faith comes by hearing, and hearing by the Word of God." It's impossible to please God without faith. But you cannot have faith until you hear; and you cannot hear the way you are supposed to hear if you have been shaped a certain way. All those who hear my messages or read my books hear the same word, but that doesn't mean they are hearing at the same level, or even hearing the same message. We understand things according to our perception; in other words, we understand according to the way we have been shaped.

For example, when we say, "You must prosper," someone here will say, "It's about time we heard a message on prosperity." Someone else will get angry and say, "They only talk about money in that church." They both hear the same words, but their shaping produces a different response to the words. It is my responsibility as a church leader not just to lead people to salvation, although that's the first step. My responsibility is to teach people how to hear because if you hear the right way, you can do the right thing.

The first section of this book will cover the demonic agendas that affect our perceptions and shape our thinking. It is imperative that we recognize these agendas that often appear as commonplace problems within the body of Christ. Once they are identified, we can begin removing these issues in order to replace them with Kingdom theology. The second section of the book will address the way the Kingdom functions, taking you step-by-step through the methodology necessary for a Kingdom mindset.

Please stop now, dear reader, and ask the Lord to give you wisdom and understanding before your proceed. If we are to be the generation that will bring the Kingdom of God, a substantial mind shift must occur. It is always difficult to embrace a new paradigm, because once your mind is set, it is a challenge to use your mind to change your mind! Nevertheless, the Holy Spirit will renew us through the transforming of our mind through the truth of God's Word!

INCREASE OF THE KINGDOM

DEMONIC AGENDAS

INCREASE OF THE KINGDOM

CHAPTER 1
TEN REASONS PROBLEMS EMERGE

Before we can begin to understand the function of the Kingdom and direct its application into our daily lives, we must first address the demonic agendas that have historically caused problems within the body of Christ and in society at large. Some might think that the issues listed below are benign, common place problems that should not be listed as "demonic." However, these problems have kept us from fully embracing the message of the Kingdom and taking dominion of the earth; these issues, whether alone or combined have stunted our growth; they've cost time, money, tears, family, and more. They have stolen, killed, and destroyed destiny and purpose, and, therefore, are very much demonic. Listed below are the primary reasons problems emerge:

1. No Leadership.
2. No Vision.
3. No Financial Understanding.
4. No Structure.
5. No Order.
6. No Competence.
7. No Quality Relationships.
8. No Generational Planning.
9. No Spiritual Depth.
10. No Understanding of the Times.

If you're going to be current in the Kingdom of God, all those things are important factors. We are going to examine each dynamic, covering a few within each chapter. We begin with the first three in this chapter: leadership, vision and money.

Leadership

Problems emerge from a lack of leadership. The lack of leadership can occur within business, church, family, government, or all of the above. Here are four facts regarding leadership:

1. Leadership is both physical and spiritual. In the physical realm, you lead your family; you lead your ministry; you lead your business; you lead your nation. You're the one who sits on the top of the rock as Moses did with lifted arms while Joshua was in the field. You lead like Joshua by walking in front of the people when crossing the river Jordan. You lead the troops as David did by killing the giant. If you don't lead, you're in trouble. So you lead physically, and you lead spiritually. When it's time to make a sacrifice, offer that sacrifice and lead as Elijah or Samuel. Like David, you worship and lead the Ark of the Covenant into the city. People must see you worship if you're a leader. So you lead physically and you lead spiritually.

2. Leadership is dimensional. Leadership is dimensional as you progress in life and your roles and functions change. For instance, if you remain, as in King David's case, on the giant killer level, you'll never be able to build a nation because all you'll be doing is killing giants. 2 Samuel 7:8 says, "Now therefore so shalt thou say unto my servant David, Thus saith the Lord of hosts, I took thee from the sheepcote, from following the sheep, to be ruler over my people, over Israel." God reminded David that he was called to be ruler and shepherd over His people, and David learned to move dimensionally. When the four giant brothers of Goliath appeared in 2 Samuel 21, the first one was named Ishbi-Benob and the last one was a freakish man who was almost 12 feet tall. He had six toes on each foot and six fingers on each hand. They'd never seen such a huge giant. The Bible says that

it was David's men that killed the giants. The fact that David didn't kill them didn't mean that he wasn't a leader; he was still the leader, but leadership is dimensional, and God had moved him into another dimension. Jesus still leads His church although He's not here physically. He's in another dimension, but He still leads His church.

3. Leadership is situational. At church, I am the leader; but if we're driving home, and there is an accident with someone sustaining an injury, I'm not leading because I can't stand the sight of blood. If I'm shaving and cut myself, I start feeling faint because I can't stand blood. Many, many times I've been to hospitals to see very sick people, and I get very lightheaded because that's not my world. Now I'll pray, and I'll speak in tongues with my eyes closed, but I'm not your man in an accident. You need a nurse or a doctor because the situation demands that.

I'm not a lawyer; I can give some counsel based on my sense of what's right and wrong but if you need some advice pertaining to legal issues, go see a lawyer. I'm not an economist; I've worked with money; I read books and know a few things here and there. But if you have a situation where you need to make massive investments of your revenues, I can't give you financial advice. You need to go see somebody who leads in that field. I'm not an architect—I did a bit of drawing and I can read a plan. I know what a corridor and a turret are; I know what a double wall is; I know those things. But if you want to build a building and ask me to be your project manager, I'm not your man. I'm the Bishop of the church, but I can't go there and command the building to come out of the ground. You need a structural engineer; a surveyor, a concrete man.

Clearly, leadership is situational. This is important for the kingdom of God, because we have church leaders in our world that think that they can do everything and think that they have to be the best in everything they do. Then, when people appear that are more qualified than they in certain areas, they tend to undervalue or demean them, instead of honoring their gift and using their knowledge and expertise. Wisdom understands that leadership is situational.

4. Leadership is critical. Without leadership, no one is going anywhere. Someone must lead. If a man doesn't embrace his role as head of the family and take responsibility for his family, difficult times will persist. Likewise, if the president of a corporation doesn't direct his business, there will be losses. History shows the travesties that occur in nations with poor leadership—those leaders that have no courage, no backbone, no integrity—the people of the nation suffer. Some suffer for decades, even centuries, all because of poor leadership. In the Book of Judges, they asked a man by the name of Jotham to be their leader. He answered, "I'm not going to be your leader." Then he told this parable:

> The trees once went out to anoint a king over them, and they said to the olive tree, 'Reign over us.' But the olive tree said to them, 'Shall I leave my abundance, by which gods and men are honored, and go hold sway over the trees?' And the trees said to the fig tree, 'You come and reign over us.' But the fig tree said to them, 'Shall I leave my sweetness and my good fruit and go hold sway over the trees?' And the trees said to the vine, 'You come and reign over us.' But the vine said to them, 'Shall I leave my wine that cheers God and men and go hold sway over the trees?' Then all the trees said to the bramble, 'You come and reign over us.' And the bramble said to the trees, 'If in good faith you are anointing me king over you, then come and take refuge in my shade, but if not, let fire come out of the bramble and devour the cedars of Lebanon.' (Judges 9:8–15, ESV)

Many people and many cultures have been so desperate to follow someone or something, that they've chosen a thorn bush to be the leader, and the results are painful. Good leadership can make or break a people and a nation; it is crucial. Jesus didn't preach and then have leaders drawn to Him; Jesus sought them out. He found leaders with the qualities He wanted and said, "Follow Me." In order to become successful, leaders must be hand-picked. They cannot be individuals you "settle for." They must be those that exhibit the qualities of leadership combined with the integrity needed to be entrusted with power. Leadership is critical.

Vision

Problems emerge from a lack of vision. Below are five components of vision:

1. Insight is a component of vision. We need insight not only into the lives of other people and situations but also we need insight regarding ourselves. It's called introspection. We need to be able to look into our lives and recognize our strengths and weaknesses. Where do we excel? Where are we efficient? Where are we insufficient? We must frequently take inventory of our lives, our families, and our ministries and recognize the areas that need attention, those areas that need to be fortified. Before we cast our vision, we must have clarity. We must know our gifts and talents, but we should also know the areas that need improvement. Every year, my wife ChiChi and I put together our ministry plans as well as our personal plans. As we process the plans for our church, we hold strategic meetings in order to recognize and utilize the gifts God has placed in our ministry. We plan according to our resources, as well as according to God's plans for our future. Vision casting involves God's promises as well as our physical resources abounding in both the material and spiritual world.

2. Foresight is another component of vision. Before you look into the future, however, you must be retrospective. Use hindsight to

look back to see all the places that you've made mistakes so that you don't repeat those mistakes. History repeats itself. We don't want to keep making the mistakes another generation made. If we're going to project our vision in foresight, we must make sure that we don't repeat the mistakes of the past.

3. Vision is prophetic. We view our future; we visualize it and see it with our spiritual eyes.

4. Vision is actual. Vision is not hypothetical. Without vision, people perish. Vision is reality; it must exist to sustain life.

5. Vision is strategic. We shouldn't submit a declaration of war if we don't have enough soldiers. We shouldn't begin construction on a tower that we don't have the finances to complete. We don't want to build a future if we haven't secured the structure to sustain it. Vision must be strategic, which means, we may need to include education seminars and on-the-job training; we may need to create policies and procedures and refine our accounting processes. We must learn how to manage resources because vision is definitely strategic.

Financial Understanding

Problems emerge from a lack of financial understanding. Many people believe a lack of money to be the issue, when the reality is that many people don't understand how money works. Some people struggle because they don't understand the system. Most people work for money, but in reality money should work for you. Regardless of how much money you have, you must learn to make it work for you, and you should start when you only have a little.

The main principle everyone should learn is that money really does grow on trees! Everyone should discover how to plant and grow their own personal money tree. For our purposes here, I'm going to give you a short summary of how that happens. For a more detailed explanation, please refer to my book entitled *Kingdom Economics* released in September 2014.

The first step in growing a money tree is the same step required to grow anything—the seed. The seed is the initial investment. The investment seed could be in the form of a college degree, a building, a house, a business, or even a ministry. The investment costs us something; we sell all we have in order to buy a field, knowing it holds a treasure. The investment seed is planted in the ground of your life.

From that seed, the root system develops. Anything without a substantial root system cannot last. It's no different in the financial world—a weak financial root will not sustain a lifetime of financial need. The financial root is developed by determining the way to acquire money, spend money, save money, and give money. How will money be handled? The way this question is answered will either be wise or foolish and will determine the strength of the root system. Below is a basic chart on how money should be handled:

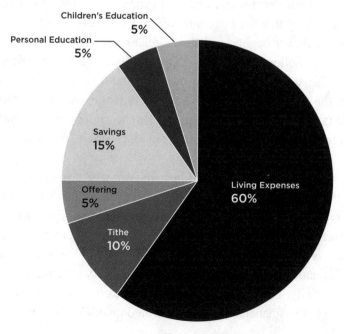

The next level of our tree is the trunk. The trunk is the support system for the entire tree. It transports resources to the branches, the leaves, and the fruit. The roots feed the trunk, and it grows and becomes the main support structure for your finances. Once your trunk becomes secure, you began to branch out and diversify. Observe how banks operate, for example. They don't just have one center; they develop branches all over the nation. It's the branches that produce the leaves, or covering, for the tree. Many people walk through life completely exposed— they don't have covering because they don't have branches producing leaves. The leaves provide covering for your life, which includes your expenses, pleasures, property, and investments. The leaves are a vital part of prosperity, but they cannot exist without the branches, and the branches can't exist without the trunk, and of course, the trunk must have a substantial root system. Success is always determined by the root system.

The money tree begins with the seed, grows with the root system, builds the trunk, expands with the branches, flourishes with the leaves, blossoms with the flowers, and then produces the long awaited fruit. It's interesting that the beginning of the fruit starts with the blossom. When the flower begins to bloom, it releases the fragrance of the next generation. Following that flower is the fruit. So many end their money tree at this stage—they eat the fruit. But the fruit is not to eat at this stage; the fruit is more seed. The first fruits are seed fruits; the seed inside is to be planted in order to start another money tree. Twenty-five years from now we'll have a forest, not just a single, fruitless tree.

When people don't understand how money works, they eat the first fruit they receive and throw away the seed. They don't take the time to harvest the seed, plant it, and grow a root system. Growing a forest demands sacrifice, which is difficult for an instant gratification society; but the sacrifice is worth it in the long run. Sacrifice teaches us how to rule financially. We must learn to use money with directed strategy and creativity. Never bury your money, but circulate and invest it to empower your financial impact. The Kingdom of God will gain traction when Believers learn key financial principles and begin to apply them. Keep in mind that the primary topic Jesus discussed was the Kingdom, and then proper relationship to money followed a close second! Could it be that these two go hand-in-hand? Problems emerge when people do not have a Biblically-based financial understanding.

INCREASE OF THE KINGDOM

CHAPTER 2:
THE IMPORTANCE OF STRUCTURE AND ORDER

Structure

Problems emerge from a lack of structure. Structure is very important. You cannot have anything meaningful or lasting without a structure. The Bible says in Revelation 13:8, "And all that dwell upon the earth shall worship him, whose names are not written in the book of life of the Lamb slain from the foundation of the world." The earth has a foundation, and the Word says that Jesus was slain from the foundation of the world. Everything must have a structure. A structure is needed for life and family, business and finance, church and ministry.

When a physical building is erected, it begins with the foundation, upon which is built the framework. If the building is to be strong and enduring, it must be a solid structure. Similarly, airplanes, cars, and other transportation vehicles must have a stable structure. Some of the items in vehicles are simply "bells and whistles" but without the framework, the superstructure, the vehicle will not be functional. For instance, a car has to have a chassis to keep all the pieces together. In order for things in the material world to be fully functional, they must have a stable structure. Likewise, everything in our lives, both material and spiritual, needs proper structure.

Lack of structure causes us to struggle. Many individuals can experience a sudden breakthrough. Perhaps it is an incredible financial opportunity with the potential to produce major revenues. Suddenly, the fruit becomes substantial, and the branches cannot sustain the weight of the fruit; thus the branch breaks. I've witnessed this in the natural. Years ago, while jogging, I saw a branch from a coconut tree lying on the ground. The coconuts were so large, so heavy, that they had broken the branch of the tree. ChiChi and I recently visited a farm and saw another similar sight. A massive branch of an avocado pear tree had broken off because the avocados were so big on the branches and heavier than the structure could bear. The fruit was bigger than the structure; thus the fruit broke the structure. I've seen this happen even more often within organizations and financial situations than I have in the natural. Once the structure is broken, it can take years to repair. In order to once again produce fruit, repair and rebuilding are necessary. And sadly, during those years of rebuilding the structure that will once again produce fruit, many years of additional fruit-bearing are lost.

In order to reap continually increasing fruit, the structure must be properly built initially. While believing for the fruit, we must maintain a solid structure, shoring up weak areas. We need to construct Kingdom models for leadership. We have to look at the Joseph model, the David model, the Daniel model—how these individuals, even in adversity and in difficult times, built structures. And those structures, if implemented today, still function very well.

Within our structures we must include long-term planning. We must put together strategic purposeful life plans for everything we do. Let's look at this concept using God's instruction book: "Now ye are the body of Christ, and members in particular. And God hath set some in the church, first apostles, secondarily prophets, thirdly teachers, after that miracles, then gifts of healings, helps, governments, diversities of tongues" (1 Corinthians 12:27,28). Paul addresses the church by saying we are members of the body of Christ. In verse 28, he tells us what the body looks like. The first parts in the superstructure of God's world are apostles, prophets and teachers. Then come "miracles, gifts of healing, helps, governments, diversities of tongues." So verse 28 frames the superstructure as to the way the church is established. It is important that we understand there is a structure by which things must be run.

I'll give you a basic view of structure in three dimensions. We are body, soul (mind, emotion, will), and spirit. That's a human being. God is known as Father, Son, and Holy Ghost. Simple. Now there are other things that He is, but Father, Son, and Holy Ghost, the three in One, is the structure of the Godhead. The structure of human beings is body, soul and spirit. We see this pattern of three's emerging in several areas of structure:

- The structure of the family: father, mother, children
- The structure of the tabernacle—the courtyard, the Holy Place, the Holiest of Holies
- The structure of a believer—faith, hope and charity
- The structure of our experience—in Him we live, in Him we move, and in Him we have our being.
- The structure of the way Jesus ministers—He's the same yesterday, today and forever.
- The structure of the anointing—priest, prophet, king
- The structure of the way God establishes His church—foolish virgin, wise virgin, Bride of Christ

It's all in three's; it's a basic three-dimensional structure. We add pieces as we go along. Any successful person or any successful thing must have a structure.

For ministry you have to have a reporting structure which is hierarchical. On the top, you have leaders and everybody else serves up. We also have what we call the wheel in the middle of the wheel in Ezekiel 10:10, "And as for their appearances, the four had one likeness, as if a wheel had been in the midst of a wheel." There is the wheel or center, then the nucleus, and everything grows out from it. That's how God functions. He's the wheel in the middle of the wheel. When the middle of the wheel turns, everything else in God's world turns. God does things in circles. For instance, the sun is in the center of our solar system. We have eight major planets, and they all orbit the sun. The sun is in the center of our solar system, and we're going around the sun.

Then the sun and its organization are going around another system, the Milky Way.

Everything within God's world is in circles. The Bible says in John 1:4, "In Him was life, and the life was the light of men." God is light. How does light move? Light moves in lines traveling at 186,000 miles per second; it never changes. Light doesn't bend, but it manifests in circles. For instance, if you stand under a street light, you see a circle, not a square. If you're wearing glasses and look into the light, you can see circles. Although light moves in straight lines, it manifests in circles because God is cyclic.

Likewise, everything in our lives is a cycle. The year is a cycle—spring, summer, autumn, and winter. The female reproductive system has a cycle—both in the animal kingdom and in the kingdom of man. Farming follows a cycle—seedtime and harvest. Life offers a time of weeping but also a time of joy. The day offers morning, noon and night. If you are currently in a night season, take heart knowing the morning will come! Everything in life is cyclical.

Structure in life should be built on a basic understanding that life is cyclical. When we build structurally, there are certain things we have to set in our lives. Ephesians 2:20 says, "…having been built upon the foundation." You must have a foundation in your life—a fundamental foundational structure. You cannot live your life without a foundation. This foundation must include your fundamental non-negotiable values—core beliefs, core values, and core purposes. Those must be set in the foundational structure of your life. The Bible says in Matthew 7 that two houses were built, one house on the rock and one house on the sand. Both houses were tested. Sand represents the philosophies of man (ever changing, ever shifting). Rock represents the foundational truths of the Bible, which include Christocentric principles. Man's ever-changing philosophies provide no foundation, so the house will not stand during the storms of life. Biblical foundations will never change; His Word has stood the test of time and is just as relevant in this hour as it has ever been, perhaps even more so. Biblical truth provides a rock-solid foundation that is immovable in even the worst of storms. Storms will come, so build your house on the rock.

The storm comes in three ways:

1. The Bible says the rain came and beat on the house. Rain represents the test of prosperity.
2. The Bible says the floods hit against the house. Floods represent demonic powers. ("When the enemy shall come in like a flood, the Spirit of the LORD shall lift up a standard against him" Isaiah 59:19b).
3. The winds blew upon the house. Winds represent the doctrines of men. Ephesians 4:14 states, "...no longer tossed to and fro by every wind of doctrine."

Without a strong foundation, the rain of prosperity can cause the house to collapse. Years ago an author wrote that the test of prosperity is one that 95% of all Christians fail. Apparently, Believers can withstand hardship and adversity, but great wealth causes hearts to turn cold. Perhaps the greatest test we must pass is the test of wealth; and perhaps that is one reason so many Believers are not wealthy—God knows they cannot pass that test.

Without a strong foundation, the floods of demonic assault can flatten your structure. Demonic attacks do happen; spiritual warfare is real. The wise Believer will build a strong foundation on the Word and be ready to employ his spiritual arsenal. Are you wearing the full armor of God?

Without a strong foundation, the fickle winds of man's philosophies will destroy the house. Recent studies show that the majority of young Christian teens abandon their faith within only weeks of attending secular universities? Why? Apparently their faith wasn't built upon the rock solid truth of God's Word. They are assaulted with atheistic, humanistic, God-hating rhetoric, and these tornadic winds destroy their faith. Structure is imperative. A strong foundation is a must, not only in our personal lives, but also within the confines of the body of Christ.

Paul shows us in Ephesians 2:20 how to build the foundation of the church. He says, "And (you) are built upon the foundation of the apostles and prophets, Jesus Christ himself being the chief corner stone." This gives us the architectural blueprint for constructing the church. First, the foundation is laid through the apostles and prophets—the apostolic and prophetic are fundamental—they provide the foundation. So many churches exist today that have no apostolic or prophetic headship. Some factions even believe apostles and prophets were for the New Testament Church only, as if God would just discard two of the five building blocks of the church! So, the apostolic and prophetic are the foundation, and Jesus Christ Himself is the cornerstone. He is the first stone in the building and the stone that holds it all together. He is the model. We model ourselves according to His building which brings structure to our lives.

God intends for us to structure everything according to His plan, modeled after Heaven itself. We see this throughout the Word. In Philippians 3:20, we read that our conversation must be in heaven, "For our conversation is in heaven; from whence also we look for the Savior, the Lord Jesus Christ." When the Lord gave Moses the tabernacle plan, He gave him a building pattern. In Exodus 25:8, 9 we see, "And let them make me a sanctuary; that I may dwell among them. According to all that I shew thee, after the pattern of the tabernacle, and the pattern of all the instruments thereof, even so shall ye make it." Everything we do on earth should be based on the pattern and the blueprint in the heavens.

Likewise, we see David share the plans for the temple to King Solomon in 1 Chronicles 28:10–12:

> *Take heed now; for the LORD hath chosen thee to build an*
> *house for the sanctuary: be strong, and do it. Then David*

*gave to Solomon his son the pattern of the porch, and
of the houses thereof, and of the treasuries thereof, and
of the upper chambers thereof, and of the inner parlors
thereof, and of the place of the mercy seat, And the pattern
of all that he had by the spirit, of the courts of the house
of the LORD, and of all the chambers round about, of the
treasuries of the house of God, and of the treasuries of the
dedicated things.*

He instructed Solomon to "build God's house according to the pattern."
Just like the tabernacles, our lives must be patterned after God's plans.
A solid structure must be in place that consists of a proper foundation,
strong steel beams, and impenetrable materials that can withstand the
tests of this life. A strong structure begins with a foundation that is built
on the Rock.

Consider this Old Testament story. Israel was delivered from Egyptian
bondage and led into the desert wilderness by Moses. In Exodus 17,
while in Horeb, the people were thirsty. God instructed Moses to strike
a rock. He did so, and water gushed from the rock. In this story, the
rock represented Christ. He became their refreshing, the satisfaction
of their thirst. As the day progressed, the enemy began to attack the
Israelites. Moses climbed to the top of a hill where he sat upon another
rock, holding his arms high. He surrendered to the rock of authority, and
consequently, the victory was won. When we submit to the authority of
the rock, we will also be refreshed from the water flowing from the rock.
In other words, if we structure our lives on the rock of Christ's headship,
he will meet our needs through His flow of resources. Structure must be
in place, must be built upon the rock, and must be built with strategy.

Without structure there is no strategy. A good strategy is a method of
logical steps that ensure a positive outcome. It pertains to organizing
systematic plans for success. If strategy is lacking, the structure is
weak. Jesus first built the structure; then He formed a strategy. The
strategy began with choosing twelve apostles who became part of the

foundation, and He put the Word in their mouths. We must build a strategy. Consider the steps below:

1. We must be problem solvers. We have the mind of Christ, and we must access this intellect. Our sanctified brains must be employed. We must think systematically and in order. For instance, marriage is about more than companionship, sex, and enjoyment. Marriage is the first step in building a family, and there needs to be a strategic plan in place. Children usually follow marriage and with them a host of additional blessings and expenses. The 21st century estimate for providing a college education for one child is approximately $147,000. If college is part of the expectation, a plan must be in place. We must be problem solvers. We must think strategically.

2. We must have the spirit of excellence. Anything worth doing is worth doing well. Proverbs 22:29 tells us, "Do you see a man who excels in his work? He will stand before kings; He will not stand before unknown men."

3. We must be disciplined. In other words, we are not going to deviate from the strategy or change in midstream. When ChiChi and I put our strategy together several years ago, that strategy meant we had to make sacrifices in some areas. Things weren't easy or convenient. We had to endure certain hardships. Now we are enjoying the sacrifices of our labor. We were disciplined not to deviate from our strategy, and it was worth it. It meant we had to walk. We structured and strategized, and now we are smiling—all the way to the bank!

4. We must build teams. We were designed for relationship. The family of man was created to work together, just as the body of Christ was structured to work in teams to represent one unified unit. In our families, we need to know one another's strengths and weaknesses. We need to capitalize on the strengths and help

one another fortify our weaknesses. We need to do the same in our businesses and our ministries. Rather than compete among ourselves, we need to honor one another's God-given gifts and utilize them for strategic implementation in building impermeable structures. For years after we began the Jabula group, I asked our pastors, "What can I do for you?" I soon discovered I was asking the wrong question. Rather than submitting a plan for strengthening the vision of the ministry, they would give me a list of material items.

In more recent years, I have employed King David's strategy. I now ask them, "What can you do for me?" That question may sound self-centered to some, but it is the right question to ask if everyone in our ministry is to align themselves with the corporate vision. If our ministry teams are focused on the vision of the house, rather than on their own personal needs, we will reach our corporate vision, and their personal visions will also be utilized in doing so. Does the question now become clearer? More purposeful? Our strategies employ key people willing to give their best in every area; people willing to offer their ideas, revenue, resources, and time. Here's the principle that Jesus used: You can never have your own ministry until you've served someone else. If you are unwilling to be faithful in little, you can never be faithful with much. It is important not to despise the day of small beginnings because this is the test for your faithfulness, your endurance. If we cannot handle small beginnings, how will we manage big breakthroughs? When someone succeeds on a large scale, it is because at some point they succeeded on a small scale.

Strong structure is imperative if we are to build anything lasting; and strategy must be utilized if we are to do so. Neither structure nor strategy will exist outside of proper order. God is a God of order—it is a fundamental part of Him and His Kingdom.

Order
Problems emerge because of a lack of order. Kingdom increase cannot occur in the midst of disorder. Order is of paramount importance, and

below are a few items that cause disorder:

1. Abnormalities in our systems cause disorder. We cannot know what an abnormality is unless we have exposure to the normal. A recent speaker at one of our conferences talked about a certain man who went to a restaurant to eat. He saw the table napkin and put it over his shoulder. He then taught his family to do the same thing. When the family went to a restaurant together, they noticed others putting the napkins in their laps, not on their shoulders. By being exposed to the normal, they realized that the way they had been taught was abnormal. Unfortunately, some people are so set in their ways, determined to live by what they've been taught (even if it is destructive or unfruitful) that they are unwilling to discard the abnormalities in their lives.

   When abnormality is discovered, adjustments must be made. I often share this story about my brother who bought a new house in the city of Houston. He had guests who were unfamiliar with the faucet fixture in the new kitchen. The guest operating the tap didn't know how to turn it on and pulled the whole lever out, causing water to spray everywhere. It was in the evening and there was no place to get a new fixture so my brother used a vise grip to turn the water off and left it there. They were so busy, they continued to use the vise grip rather than repair the faucet.

   Several weeks later, Pastor ChiChi and I went on vacation to be with them, and my brother still had not repaired the faucet. My brother showed ChiChi how to turn on the water with the vise grip. He was teaching her how to function in abnormality. When I saw it, I just thought it was a new American thing! I had not seen the faucet function normally, so I accepted the abnormality. For days while we were there, we functioned in abnormality. This illustration shows us how such can be passed from one generation to the next without anyone realizing they are functioning abnormally.

If order is to exist, abnormality must be corrected. For some, a normal weekend might look like this: "Friday nights we drink; we fight; we close the bar; we hit our wives; the children scatter; wife runs to her parents in her nightie; spends the weekend there. Sunday we get up with a hangover; we go and we ask the parents to forgive us; we kiss the wife; we bring her back; we have another baby a year later." Some people live in situations like I just described, completely convinced it's normal, when in reality a life like that is completely dysfunctional; it's abnormal.

I've seen churches function in abnormality. Some ministries exploit their staff and their congregation. The lead pastor does it, so the others follow. It becomes a characteristic of the church or the ministry, and even though it is wrong and abnormal, it continues. If abnormality exists and is not corrected, it continues with the next generation.

2. Secondly, we must address dysfunction. Dysfunctional behavior occurs when a person is lacking a rational ability to deal with a certain situation. Dysfunction is usually created by abuse or repetitive negative exposure that produces an illogical emotional response to a typical situation. For example, a woman gives her husband money to pay the rent, but instead he uses the money for something else. She questions him about the rent, and he responds with an angry voice, "Are you accusing me of something?" Rather than respond to a simple, reasonable question, the man reacts with illogical emotion. He displays dysfunctional behavior. Often people get offended because they haven't learned how to deal with issues and pain of their past. Everything, every situation, every conversation becomes a personal assault. They have a basic inability to look at some situations through a rational lens.

Essentially, dysfunction is a weakness that needs to be overcome. One of the best ways to overcome weakness is to make it known.

James 5:16 tells us, "Confess your faults one to another that you may be healed." We need to expose our weaknesses whether they be financial, familial, sexual, or other. As counter intuitive as it may seem, vulnerability actually brings strength. The devil thrives in the darkness. He wants to keep everything hidden because the darkness gives him continual power over people. The Bible says in Hebrews 12:1, "We must lay aside every weight and the sin which so easily besets us." When we bring our weaknesses into the light, and confess our sins, they no longer have power over us.

3. Finally, we must do away with disorder. Disorder exists in so many places that many times it can be overwhelming. I suggest starting in your home. Have a rack for your keys and put them there every time you come through the door. Keep a box for your receipts, a file for your bills. Hang up the clothes in your closet! People waste so much time looking for things. Lost items are a clear sign of disorder. Many countries have cities full of disorder. With one panoramic look, litter, graffiti, weeds, and stray animals come into view. Men stand in the street spitting, urinating, drinking, and loitering—total disorder everywhere. Other countries have orderly cities. Take Singapore, for instance. People are fined for spitting chewing gum in the street. Singapore has a sign posted that says, "All crimes with drugs are punishable by death. All crimes with guns are punishable by death. All sexual crimes are punishable by death. All spitting in the street is fined and receive 12 cuts with a cane." When you enter Singapore, you must sign a form that states you understand these laws.

If someone is caught with drugs in Singapore, there's no court hearing. He will be sentenced to death because he read the statement, signed the statement, and then broke the law. Years ago, a young man was found with drugs in his suitcase and was sentenced to death. The Prime Minister of Britain appealed for clemency, as did other human rights group. No clemency was given. The only concession Singapore gave was that his mother was allowed to hold his hand for a few minutes prior to his execution. Singapore has created a society of order. The young man brought disorder by breaking the law. It cost him his life. Though this is an extreme example, we see that disorder can bring great destruction.

Begin dealing with the disorder in your life. Begin at home. Then look at your relationships. If you borrow someone's car, fill it with gas before you return it. If you make an appointment, arrive early, not late. Keep a calendar of events. Honor your word and honor other people's time. Bring order into your life, and your life will flourish.

I am a naturally untidy person, but I refuse to allow disorder in my life. There was a time I'd open my suitcase and the contents would fall onto the floor in a disheveled heap. I now pack my suitcase with great deliberation. I color code all my shoes in plastic bags, packed together, marked, and numbered. I do the same with all my clothes. I must have order in my life if I am to succeed.

Man was not created until the sixth day. First, God put everything into order. Man could not be created in the chaos. The first thing man witnessed was an orderly earth. If man had been introduced to disorder, it would have become natural in his life. Disorder is not natural and should never be accepted as such.

We overcome disorder by taking dominion. The steps to dominion are as follow:

1. Gifts produce service. A musician serves in music; a teacher teaches; and a person good with toddlers serves in the nursery.

2. Service produces credibility. The more one serves, the more credibility he earns. Credibility cannot come without service.

Elisha followed and served Elijah, receiving his mantle of a prophet when Elijah was taken up into heaven in 2 Kings 2. Elisha's service produced credibility, and he received a double portion. Joshua served Moses for forty years so, when it was time to pass the baton, it went to Joshua because his service produced credibility.

3. Credibility produces influence. A pastor of an 8,000 member church called me a while back. He said, "Bishop, can you please help me find someone to take over my church; I need a pastor to take over my church." Then he said, "Because I know you, I know you'd never recommend anyone ineligible." He knew he could trust my recommendation because he has seen me serve, and my service has produced credibility. My credibility has influence.

4. Influence produces atmosphere. I traveled to a conference some years ago, and my suitcase didn't arrive. I usually don't travel in jeans unless I'm on vacation; I try to travel in a sports jacket or suit and tie so that I look great, because I rarely travel places where someone doesn't know me. However, this particular trip I had worn skinny jeans, a Liverpool soccer jersey, boots, and my hat; and my suitcase was lost! The flight arrived late, so I had to go immediately to the service. I was standing in the corner at the airport, waiting for the bus driver to pick me up, and I saw these guys stepping out of the elevator dressed so smartly.

I knew they were going to the service, and one of the guys came to me and said, "How are you doing?" I said, "Oh, I'm fine." He said, "I don't recognize the accent." I said, "I'm from Africa." He said, "Yeah, we've got a preacher from Africa preaching for us tonight. What are you doing tonight?" I said, "I'm going to church." He said, "Where are you going?" So I mentioned the church; and he said, "Yeah, we've got a preacher from Africa; he's preaching there tonight. You have to hear this guy."

"What country are you from?" I said, "Zimbabwe." He said, "This guy's from Zimbabwe. Maybe you know him; his name is Tudor Bismark." I said, "I'm Tudor Bismark." He said, "Hey, the preacher's here! Let's take pictures." Until he knew my name, the atmosphere remained unchanged. My name has come to carry influence, and that influence changes the atmosphere. I have been in so many conferences and watched great people of influence walk into the room. Just their presence changes the entire atmosphere.

5. Atmosphere produces change.
6. Change produces seed.
7. Seed produces fruit.
8. Fruit produces dominion.

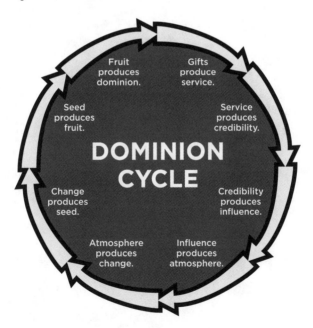

Embrace the dominion cycle. Start at step one and be faithful; and watch the disorder begin to dissipate from your life and the lives of those in your sphere of influence. Once order exists, God can direct resources into our lives, businesses, ministries, and more.

CHAPTER 3

THE IMPORTANCE OF RELATIONSHIPS & GENERATIONAL PLANNING

Relationships are so important in the Kingdom of God. I will dedicate a large portion of this chapter to the subject of relationship, first discussing the importance of quality relationships, then looking at the types of relationships to avoid and those you want to have, and the levels within relationships. I will then conclude this chapter with a brief look at the importance of generational planning. There's a great deal covered within this chapter, so grab your highlighter!

The Importance of Quality Relationships

Problems arise when quality relationships have not been established. Individuals have each been endowed with unique gifts and talents, and it is imperative to connect with them and connect them to each other. Every ministry, every business, every country, every nation, every kingdom, and every family is only as strong as its gifted people. We cannot be greater than our gifted people.

There are times when we are endowed with an immense anointing that allows us to do mighty exploits. Anointing came on David when he killed Goliath with a stone. However, after Goliath fell, an army of Philistines with swords remained. The stones were used for Goliath, but Goliath's sword was used for the remainder of the battle. We must understand how to engage all of the resources God gives us.

At some point, we have to raise our gift level and our skill level. God can anoint me as a preacher; but if I don't improve my skill—read more, study more, and go into the Word of God more, I'll lack substance. I will be a sounding brass or tinkling cymbal, saying the same things over and over again without any new revelation. We must improve our skill level. Everyone has gifts, but those gifts must be developed and constantly improved upon. We have intelligent, brilliant, academic kids who never get a chance to go to school. They are intelligent, but they are limited if their skill level never improves. If people with great potential never tap into their gifts and skills, honing them for ultimate effectiveness, their potential will never be reached. This is true of everything in our lives.

Since we are only as strong as the gifted people in our lives and as effective as our powerful and strong people, we must take the time to develop those areas. The Bible says in Acts 7:22, "And Moses was learned in all the wisdom of the Egyptians, and was mighty in words and in deeds." Moses was chosen by God to deliver the Israelites from Egyptian bondage. God educated Moses from birth, having him raised within Pharaoh's own household. He became intimately acquainted with Egyptian society, trained in their customs and ways. In Pharaoh's house, he gained the knowledge of Egypt. Moses became mighty in word and deed. God specifically orchestrated Moses' development, and he became a major deliverer. Likewise, if we are to be major deliverers, we must purposely improve our skills.

Daniel was a man of prayer. He often prayed all day. Daniel 9:4:5 says,

> *And I prayed unto the LORD my God, and made my*
> *confession, and said, O Lord, the great and dreadful*
> *God, keeping the covenant and mercy to them that love*
> *him, and to them that keep his commandments; We have*
> *sinned, and have committed iniquity, and have done*
> *wickedly, and have rebelled, even by departing from*
> *thy precepts and from thy judgments: Neither have we*
> *hearkened unto thy servants the prophets, which spake in*
> *thy name to our kings, our princes, and our fathers, and to*
> *all the people of the land.*

He made deep supplications with sackcloth and ashes. The Bible then tells us that Gabriel, the archangel, came and stood next to him. Daniel 9:21, 22 says, "Yea, whiles I was speaking in prayer, even the man Gabriel, whom I had seen in the vision at the beginning, being caused to fly swiftly, touched me about the time of the evening oblation. And he informed me, and talked with me, and said, O Daniel, I am now come forth to give thee skill and understanding." Daniel had served over a period of 40 years in Babylon; at the time of this angelic visitation he was serving in his fourth administration. He had been noted as a man with great skill, highly distinguished among many. He had great wisdom and many respected him; yet the angel came to give him even more skill and understanding. Our lives are filled with times and seasons, and we are foolish to think we have acquired all the knowledge and skill we will need for our lives. We need to continually grow in wisdom and understanding in order to competently face the future.

Many times I hear people praying for God to give them a big car; then I see they can't look after their bicycle. If you can't look after your bicycle, you'll never look after a car. If you can't manage your Mazda, you can't look after a Mercedes. If you can't look after a rented apartment, you'll never manage a three-bedroom house. If you're struggling with a three-bedroom house, you'll never be able to manage a six-bedroom house.

I remember an event that occurred many years ago that was a life changer for me. ChiChi and I had a telephone disconnected for non-payment. We allowed people to use our phone, and they had run up the bill and not reimbursed us. Consequently, the phone company disconnected our service. A lady in our church was employed at the phone company and after a long process, she was able to restore our phone. She contacted me and said, "Pastor B., can you come to the office and sign a new contract?" She was a member of our church, and I was her pastor, but when I went in to sign, she said to me, "Now, look after it!" She was right to chide me; I could not get offended because it was challenging for her to have the phone restored and a painstaking task for ChiChi and me to pay the balance of what we owed.

When you have been given a gift, you have to look after it. As I've watched some of Kathryn Kuhlman's videos, I've learned that she carefully protected her gift and her anointing. She would not allow people to contaminate it.

Any person who's going to be significant in the Kingdom of God has to improve his skill level. The Bible says that when Daniel and his protégés, Meshach, Shadrach, and Abednego came to the city of Babylon to live there and serve Nebuchadnezzar, God helped them survive: "As for these four children, God gave them knowledge and skill in all learning and wisdom: and Daniel had understanding in all visions and dreams" (Daniel 1:17, ESV).

It takes knowledge and skill to go to the next level. We are only as strong as our gifts. The reason the body of Christ struggles is because we don't have skilled, gifted people in the right places. The Bible says in Psalm 33:3 to "Sing unto him a new song; play skillfully with a loud noise." When our praises come before the Lord, they should be played skillfully. Skillfully—because the skillful player will bring a quality anointing in their lives.

In 2 Chronicles 2:7–8, the temple is being built. It says, "Send me now, therefore, a man, cunning, (skilled) to work in gold, in silver, in brass, in iron, in purple, in crimson, in blue, and that can skillfully grave with the cunning men that are with me in the tribe of Judah in the city of Jerusalem, whom David, my father, did provide." Solomon wanted men who were skillful, and then he named the areas where people are gifted. All of those things—gold, silver, brass, iron, purple, crimson, blue,— are metaphors for certain levels of gifting within the church and in the body. Gold represents deity, so we need people who understand God issues. Silver is atonement, so people are needed who understand what the blood of Jesus can do. Brass symbolizes repentance and judgment;

those are people who can release judgment within the earth. Purple signifies things of royalty. We need people who can deal with royal issues and move us from poverty. One reason we struggle is because there's a lack of skill and giftedness.

Problems emerge because of a lack of quality relationships. You are who you choose to associate with. The old adage or cliché, "Birds of a feather flock together," is true. A very well-known ministry friend of ours was sharing recently with our pastoral team. He said that when he is going to promote an individual, that person must meet a certain criteria in order to qualify. The first requirement, of course, is skill and competence level, but another one of the things they watch very carefully is who that individual associates with. Who do they have lunch with after church on Sunday? Who do they go to the gym with? Who do they enjoy being with for recreation? If you have someone who says they are with you but continue to hang out with people who are against you, then they're not for you. That's the bottom line, because you are who you run with. So, in my life, there are certain relationships that I've had to sever because some of those relationships had a negative effect on my life.

A Few Examples of People to Avoid:
1. **Toxic people.** A synonym for "toxic" is "poisonous," and the toxicity levels in certain people are quite astounding. People with pervasive negative attitudes will infiltrate the atmosphere and suffocate anything positive in our lives.

2. **Critical people.** Critical people will find fault in everything; they cannot be satisfied. They are quick to identify a problem, but never offer a solution. Critical people are prideful people—those that can easily see the speck in someone else's eye, while completely oblivious to the beam in their own. Constructive criticism is a positive thing and is not something offered by critical people. I have been offered constructive criticism throughout my life and have been grateful for the input. One Sunday, during a message,

I said something about my wife. When I got home from church, my parents were at the house waiting for me. I said, "Hi, Mom and Dad. Would you like some tea or lunch?" They said, "Tudor, we didn't come to eat. We didn't even come for tea." They said, "What you said today in the pulpit, about your wife, is unacceptable. Don't ever do that again." It stunned me; I was trying to think what I had said. My parents continued, "What you said cheapened your wife and will cause people to disrespect her. Don't ever do that again." Then they got up and jumped in the car and left.

I was floored. It was one of those services that I thought was really good but was actually not so great. It stunned me. Later, when ChiChi came home, I apologized for what I had said. She didn't think what I said was horrible but thought it could become so if the behavior continued. The next day I went to see my parents and apologized to them. Later, I apologized to a group of leaders in our church. I didn't want my inappropriate comment to open the door for others. I was in the wrong, and it was good to be criticized. Constructive criticism is good and necessary. Critical people are not constructive; they are just critical. The difference between the two is obvious.

I may give my worship leader specific feedback regarding the songs he chooses. He should know my preferences. However, I'm not going to support people who complain about everything: "He's too loud; he uses too much bass; we need different songs." Criticism needs to be specific and it needs to be constructive.

3. **Sarcastic people.** Sarcasm has become a mainstay in modern culture, but it should not be tolerated. It is an imitation of real humor and is cutting and derogatory. Sarcasm is simply another form of criticism, disguised as a joke. I once heard someone say that the spirit realm doesn't recognize sarcasm; that words are taken at face value. God help us if this is true.

4. Pessimistic people. Every situation offers us two perspectives— one of triumph and one of defeat. Pessimistic people always assume defeat. They are not just cautious; they are fearful. They take negativity to a greater extreme and bring great discouragement to those around them. Pessimistic people do not have an accurate understanding of the goodness of God. They never take risks because they always expect the worst outcome. A pessimist will say, "Don't do it; we're going to die." The reality is that we might die, or we may live and live more fully! Many believe cheerleaders at sports games are simply ornamental, and perhaps they have evolved into such. However, studies have shown that men actually perform better when being cheered. We all need encouragement, not negative pessimistic blabbering!

Avoid relationships that fall into the categories above. Cultivate the following relationships:

1. Winners. Run with someone who is a winner and an achiever. Sometimes it's very difficult to have access to somebody who is a constant winner, but you can run with them informally. Watch them from a distance and emulate what they do. You can learn from the way they do things.

Take David and Jonathan for example. Saul and Jonathan were the only ones in Israel who had swords, and Jonathan was very skilled with that sword:

> *And Jonathan said to his armor-bearer, "Come up after me, for the LORD has given them (the Philistines) into the hand of Israel." Then Jonathan climbed up on his hands and feet, and his armor-bearer after him. And they fell before Jonathan, and his armor-bearer killed them after him. And that first strike, which Jonathan and his armor-bearer made, killed about twenty men (1 Samuel 14:12–14, ESV).*

Jonathan was slightly older, and David began to learn from him. 1 Samuel 18:24 tells us that Jonathan and David made a covenant together: "Then Jonathan made a covenant with David, because he loved him as his own soul. And Jonathan stripped himself of the robe that was on him and gave it to David, and his armor, and even his sword and his bow and his belt." David got Jonathan's sword. David was running with the winner. David had such a connection with Jonathan that when he died in 2 Samuel 9, David remembered Jonathan's family and restored Mephibosheth, Jonathan's son, to the royal palace.

Look for winners in your life. They don't have to be relationships that you can touch immediately. Long-term, you'll eventually get to meet some of those people. In my own life, I have had the desire to meet and work with certain people. One of them is an extremely well-known Christian motivational speaker.

Several years ago, I was one of the speakers at a conference in West Palm Beach, Florida with this famous speaker and author. The host of the service was a very nervous young man who seemed a little disoriented. He and I were the only speakers at the conference, so the young man said, "Our first speaker tonight is (this famous man). He'll be speaking for 30 minutes." Then he said, "Our keynote speaker that's rocking the world all the way from Zimbabwe is Bishop Tudor Bismark. He is in the house and he's our keynote speaker." The famous speaker/author just tapped me on my knee and said, "You go for it, son; you go for it." I know he has told that story around the world because at that point, I hadn't written a book, and I was certainly not as well-known as he. He had written over 50 books. At that point, our church was just breaking a thousand; he had pastored a church of several tens of thousands and had spoken to world leaders in every economic forum. Now here was our little host screaming that the keynote speaker is an ant from Zimbabwe!

After the famous gentlemen spoke—he spoke for an hour and 25 minutes—he came to me and he said, "Look, I know you're the keynote speaker, but I cannot stay for your session. I have an early morning flight." I put an offering in his hand and I said, "Please forgive me and please pray for me." He just winked at me and said, "You go get them," and he walked out. In my life, I've desired to be around people like that, and God has opened doors for me at strange places to make that happen.

I look for people I feel are winners that I want to be around. I visit their websites and if they're in the area, I'll pay my own way to go there and spend 15 or 20 minutes with them. I don't go to get anything tangible or physical from them but just to get an impartation of their wisdom, their life, and their experience.

Recently I had the privilege of meeting Matthew Ashimolowo, Sr. Pastor of Kingsway International Christian Centre in London. ChiChi and I were going up the stairs, and somebody tapped me on the shoulder; it was his son, Toby. I said, "What are you doing here? I'm supposed to meet you for breakfast tomorrow." He said, "No, my dad's here." I said, "I'd love to see him."

So ten minutes later, we got a call and Pastor Matthew asked me to come to his room. I sat there for an hour with him and he said to me, "You have such excellent material; you have such a systematic way of presenting, line on line. What you say has great depth." He continued, "Every sermon that you preach is a book. But I don't see the books. Some of your stuff that I've been reading is years ahead. What you need to do is organize a week in which you bring an audience into a room and teach what you know and make recordings." So I listened and followed his suggestions. We have to run with winners.

2. **Spiritual people.** Don't run with carnal people. Run with spiritual people because spirit transmits spirit.

3. Wise People. Wise people possess both knowledge and understanding. They walk in revelation and have the ability to see things others don't see. We need to surround ourselves with wise people.

4. Experienced People. Unfortunately, Western society idolizes youth and has created a general disdain for the elderly. In other cultures, and throughout history, the elders were revered and acknowledged for the life they had lived, the experience they had gained, and the wisdom they had to offer. The Bible tells us to learn from our elders—that older women should teach younger women, that younger prophets and other ministers should be mentored by the older, more experienced. Words of knowledge and prophetic revelations can come by the Spirit through people of any age; however, godly wisdom and counsel often come from those in our lives who have learned through time and experience.

So, as a general guideline we want relationships in our lives that consist of wise, spiritual, experienced winners! We want to surround ourselves with people worthy of our admiration, people who have engaged in life, fought some battles, and won some victories! The Bible tells us, "Where there is no counsel, the people fall; But in the multitude of counselors there is safety" (Proverbs 11:14, NKJV).

In addition to understanding types of people, we must also understand levels of relationship. When we develop relationships, either in a church or business venue, there are three levels that must be observed:

1. Allegiance is the first level. When we enter into an allegiance, we pledge to watch their back. We honor them, never speak badly about them, and always believe the best. When gossip circulates, we don't participate in it, nor do we believe what is being said. Rather, we call them, report the gossip, assure them that we believe the best, and tell them we are praying for them. When we have an allegiance with someone, we let them know

if we see their kids involved in something they shouldn't be. We look out for one another. We pledge loyalty to them, committing ourselves to their best interest.

2. Alliance is the next level. Alliances are important because when we make an alliance with someone, it means that we are going to support them in certain things. In other words, if there's a war declared against them, we join forces with them, as their allies to help them win the war. The Old Testament is filled with wars, nations attacking one another, cities being conquered and taken. Some nations were allies and would help other nations during the wars. In 2 Chronicles 14:9, one million Ethiopians came against Israel, and her allies stood with her during that attack. As a side note, the Bible tells us that those who stand with Israel will be blessed, and those that come against her will be cursed. As we are considering our personal allies, we might do well to pray that our nations choose their alliances wisely.

3. Covenant is the last and highest level of relationship. Even within covenant relationships, there are various levels. Not every covenant is on the same level. The first form of covenant is the handshake of fellowship. Always offer your hand before you give your heart. When we extend to each other the right hand of fellowship, we are exposing our hand. The hand represents war and work. In other words, our covenant says, "I'll work for you and with you; I'll go to war for you and with you." That's the right hand of fellowship.

My wife, ChiChi, and I are on the highest covenant level. We are transparent and accountable with one another, trusting one another explicitly. In addition we share a level of covenant only available between husband and wife; we are sexually intimate, and it signifies that we hold the deepest kind of covenant. We are connected in a bond that God Himself established in the covenant of marriage. We love each other and are committed to one another beyond our commitments to any other human being. Only our covenant with God is stronger. We share our most intimate thoughts and feelings and hold no secrets from each other. However, there are things I do not tell her. I know it sounds like I'm contradicting myself, so let me explain.

If there is a challenge, for example, in the ministry in which someone is doing something that's hurtful, I'm not going to tell her. Even though ChiChi and I have no secrets, I know it's going to harm her. I'm not doing it intentionally to keep stuff from her; I'm just doing it to protect her. She will do the same thing for me. Once a relative told me that they didn't like my wife. I wouldn't tell her that; I wouldn't tell her because it would hurt her and it could bring animosity toward this relative. Chances are, there could be a reconciliation between them; so it's better to keep some things to myself. In terms of the way we live our lives, however, we have no secrets. For anything we're buying, we're spending, what we're doing, we have no secrets. The highest level of relationships, then, is that level of intimacy.

We now understand the kind of relationships we should cultivate, the kind we should avoid, and the levels within our relationships. Within our understanding of relationships, we must consider our families and the legacy we are leaving the next generation.

Generational Planning

Problems emerge from a lack of generational planning. Genesis 18:17–19 says, "And the Lord said, 'Shall I hide from Abraham what I am doing, since Abraham shall surely become a great and mighty nation....For I have chosen him that he may command his children and his household after him, that they keep the way of the Lord, to do righteousness and justice....'"

God knew Abraham would teach his children and his grandchildren. In other words, there was a generational plan. So God is the God of

Abraham and the God of Isaac and the God of Jacob. Take a look at Genesis 21:1, 2, 5: "And the Lord visited Sarah as he had said, and the Lord did unto Sarah as he had spoken. For Sarah conceived, and bare Abraham a son in his old age, at the set time of which God had spoken to him. …. And Abraham was an hundred years old, when his son Isaac was born unto him."

In Chapter 23:1, Sarah died at the age of 127 years old. Abraham was 137 years old, and Isaac was 37 years old. Isaac married Rebekah (Genesis 24:67) and later in Genesis 25:20, we are told he was 40 years old, so that makes Abraham 140 years old. Rebekah then conceived.

Let's read Genesis 25:22–24:

> *And the children struggled together within her; and she said, If it be so, why am I thus? And she went to enquire of the LORD. And the LORD said unto her, Two nations are in thy womb, and two manner of people shall be separated from thy bowels; and the one people shall be stronger than the other people; and the elder shall serve the younger. And when her days to be delivered were fulfilled, behold, there were twins in her womb.*

The twins, Jacob and Esau, were born when Isaac was 60 years old, which meant Abraham was 160 years. Here you have two entities—one that will last for generations and one that will not. Esau's children are basically unknown. But Jacob's sons are Reuben, Simeon, Levi, Judah, Asher, Issachar, Naphtali, Dan, Gad, Zebulon, Joseph, and Benjamin. We know those boys and we know their tribes because Abraham planned generationally.

In Genesis 25:7, the Bible says, "These are the days of Abraham's life…" —so he died when he was 175 years old. If Abraham was 175 years old, it means Isaac was 75 years old. The twins, Jacob and Esau, were 15 which means Abraham had 15 years with those twins. Remember, God said I can't hide anything from Abraham because he has a generational plan so I'm going to reveal to him all things.

Now Abraham's grandson, Jacob, had a dream at a place called Luz (Bethel) described in Genesis 28:20–22:

> *And Jacob vowed a vow, saying, If God will be with me, and will keep me in this way that I go, and will give me bread to eat, and raiment to put on so that I come again to my father's house in peace; then shall the LORD be my God: And this stone, which I have set for a pillar, shall be God's house: and of all that thou shalt give me I will surely give the tenth unto thee.*

Jacob made a vow to God that, if He would bless him wherever he went, he would give a tenth, or tithe, back to Him. Where do you think he learned about paying tithes? His grandfather taught him because Abraham was a tither in Genesis 14. These are important principles.

We need to plan for our children and our grandchildren. Even if you are single and childless, you still need a plan for your family. You have to plan now, before you have children, because when you do, it's too late.

The instruction in Proverbs 13:22 is very clear. It says: "A good man leaveth an inheritance to his children's children...." That takes long-term planning. Generational planning starts with a plan for your life, a plan for your family, and a plan for your ministry/business. What is the world going to look like in the next generation? Ten years from now, life as we know it on earth will not be lived in the same way. Recently I was sitting next to a man on a flight. He said, "I want to show you something." He then proceeded to demonstrate how he could use his phone to access all the surveillance cameras in every room of his home. He could control the heat, the air conditioner, and even the music! Technology moves at an uncatchable speed. Dramatic changes are right around the corner. If we don't have a plan, the system will plan for us! We must be intentional about our future and plan accordingly.

INCREASE OF THE KINGDOM

CHAPTER 4:
SPIRITUAL DEPTH & UNDERSTANDING SEASONS

Problems emerge from a lack of spiritual depth. The previous issues we discussed are issues that exist in the world of objectivity and are relevant even in the business world. As Believers we must launch out a little deeper, beyond objectivity, and address the most important aspect in our lives—our spirituality.

On a national level, history shows us that, when a nation loses its spiritual epicenter, it is headed for destruction. A nation must have a spiritual hub and maintain spiritual sensitivity or it opens itself up to tremendous corruption, sexual decay, and rampant evil. I recently heard a psychologist address some of the issues facing America. He discussed the challenges America is encountering in the drug culture, with gun violence and sexual perversion among others. He identified the struggles as a result of America's shifting spiritual climate. America once had a godly epicenter, a strong Biblical foundation, but that foundation has been eroding for centuries.

Every nation that has a Godly spiritual hub or center has a guiding compass. The nation's level of sensitivity to immorality will be determined by its spiritual hub. When a Godly spiritual center is missing from a nation, people gravitate toward animalistic behaviors. They adopt a "survival of the fittest" mentality. The strong prey on the weak; personal interests are satisfied without consideration of the welfare of others. The rich and powerful who rule manipulate the system to their maximum benefit.

If a nation is to adequately address the issues of humanity, it must have a strong Godly spiritual epicenter. Without a moral compass, people will perish. Judges 21:23 tells us: "In those days there was no king in Israel: every man did that which was right in his own eyes." Israel had no Godly spiritual epicenter; consequently, everyone did that which was right in their own eyes. Of course, this course of action brings only destruction. Every human being has a different method of thought. Some are ruled by logic, others by emotions. Some are leaders; some are followers. Every mind has a belief system; every belief system has a shaper; every shaper has an agenda. People are shaped in different ways; consequently they approach life from many angles and employ varied methodologies. Without a moral foundation, a Godly spiritual compass, people are dangerous, and chaos ensues.

There was a situation in Las Vegas some time ago in which a person left a bag of money in cash, about $160,000, in a random cab. The taxi driver drove off. When the taxi driver realized that this person had left the bag of money, he went back to the hotel, looked for the person, and gave the money back, without taking anything out of it. The man who lost it had already resigned in his mind that the money was gone because he couldn't remember the number of the cab and was astonished that the cab driver returned all of the money. The cab driver had a moral compass; he did the right thing! Some might have looked at the bag of money as a financial breakthrough or "a blessing." But if we have a Godly, solid spiritual foundation, we recognize the right course of action and follow it.

Recently I made a purchase, and a young lady gave me change. She mistakenly gave me about $80 too much, so I said to her, "My sister, you've done the wrong thing." She wanted to argue with me because she thought I was challenging her, but I was only advising her that she wasn't giving me the right change. She would have been short in the cash register. Taking something that doesn't belong to us is stealing; it's not a "financial breakthrough." We must walk in honesty and integrity and choose to stand for morality. Choosing right comes from having a strong Godly spiritual epicenter.

People lack spiritual depth for several reasons:

1. **There is a lack of the prophetic dimension.** The prophetic dimension is essential in our growth. Let's look at two different words—*logos* and *rhema*. The word *logos* means plan or blueprint. John 1:1 says, "In the beginning was the Word," which was the thought, the idea, the plan, or the blueprint. Then in John 1:14, "The word was made flesh..." That's the *rhema* word. The plan has to be given expression, manifestation, and life. That plan is prophetic.

From the very beginning, God in His *logos*, in His plan, spoke the *rhema*, the prophetic. He tells us in Genesis 3:15 that a Messiah is coming: "And I will put enmity between thee and the woman, and between thy seed and her seed; it shall bruise thy head, and thou shalt bruise his heel."

Four thousand years down the road from that first prophecy in Genesis, Galatians 4:4 says, "When the fullness of time was come, God sent forth His Son, made of a woman, made under the law." So what was once a *logos* word became a *rhema* word. Your prophetic dimension is very important.

The Bible clearly says in 1 Corinthians 14:31 that, "Ye may all prophesy one by one, that all may learn, and all may be comforted." That doesn't make you a prophet, but it does, however, put the *rhema* word of God in your mouth.

Romans 10:8 says, "The word is nigh thee, even in thy mouth...." That's the word of faith which we release. In Romans 4:17, we "... call those things which be not as though they were." Hebrew 10: 23 tells us to "... hold fast the confession of our faith for He is faithful that promised." The prophetic dimension is important. Anytime a nation or people lose their prophetic dimension, they go back to the study of history books. That will cause them to "fossilize" and become a historical statistic. It brings death, rather than life.

Read this passage to see how the prophetic word gives life to dry bones:

> *The hand of the LORD was upon me, and he brought*
> *me out in the Spirit of the LORD and set me down in*
> *the middle of the valley; it was full of bones. And he*
> *led me around among them, and behold, there were*
> *very many on the surface of the valley, and behold,*
> *they were very dry. And he said to me, "Son of man,*
> *can these bones live?" And I answered, "O Lord GOD,*
> *YOU KNOW." Then he said to me, "Prophesy over these*
> *bones, and say to them, O dry bones, hear the word*
> *of the LORD. Thus says the Lord GOD to these bones:*
> *Behold, I will cause breath to enter you, and you shall*
> *live. And I will lay sinews upon you, and will cause*
> *flesh to come upon you, and cover you with skin, and*
> *put breath in you, and you shall live, and you shall*
> *know that I am the LORD (Ezekiel 37:1–6, ESV).*

We have to be prophetic and speak the *rhema* word of life to the lifeless things in our lives. Psalms 118:17 gives a life-giving prophetic word: "I shall not die, but live, and declare the works of the LORD." Using the prophetic doesn't mean you're going crazy, shaking your hand and shouting, "The Spirit is on me; the Spirit is on me…." Being prophetic means you must understand the process and power of releasing a *rhema* word into your present and into your future. There is a prophetic dimension which must be creatively spoken and released.

Prophetic words must be spoken out of our mouths. Prophetic words from our mouths bring completion to the things in our life. They help us finish what we've begun. God is always faithful to complete the work He starts within us, but we must cooperate with the process.

2. **There is a lack of faith.** Hebrews 11:6 tells us, "But without faith it is impossible to please him: for he that cometh to God must believe that he is, and that he is a rewarder of them that diligently seek him." So then, the walk we have is a walk of faith. Many times when you go through a test or trial, it's a trying of your faith. The trying of your faith comes in several ways:

a) **God allows a demonic attack on your life.** 1 Peter 4:12 says, "Beloved, think it not strange concerning the fiery trial which is to try you, as though some strange thing happened unto you...." James 1:2–6,8 goes on to say:

> *My brethren, count it all joy when ye fall into divers temptations; Knowing this, that the trying of your faith worketh patience. But let patience have her perfect work, that ye may be perfect and entire, wanting nothing. If any of you lack wisdom, let him ask of God, that giveth to all men liberally, and upbraideth not; and it shall be given him. But let him ask in faith, nothing wavering. For he that wavereth is like a wave of the sea driven with the wind and tossed....A double minded man is unstable in all his ways.*

So first, don't think it's strange when you go through trials. When the trying of your faith comes, count it all joy! It serves a purpose—that you might be perfect and entire, wanting nothing! The first area of your faith being tried is by the demonic world.

b) **God does test, regardless of what some may think.** He wanted to see if Abraham loved him so He gave him a son.

Then when his son was 16, read what God said in Genesis 22:1,2:

And it came to pass after these things, that God did tempt Abraham, and said unto him, Abraham: and he said, Behold, here I am. And he said, Take now thy son, thine only son Isaac, whom thou lovest, and get thee into the land of Moriah; and offer him there for a burnt offering upon one of the mountains which I will tell thee of.

God told Abraham to sacrifice his son and didn't even tell him which mountain to go to! God just said to travel. When he arrived at a certain place after three days, he saw several mountains. When he finally found the mountain, he didn't know the spot on the mountain. So all that way, Abraham was being tested; but all that way, he believed. The Bible says in Romans 4:20, "And Abraham staggered not at the promise of God." He staggered not at the promise of God because he trusted God.

So God will allow you to be tested. He will put something before you to see if it's really in your heart. Hebrews 11:6 tells us, "Without faith, it is impossible to please God." Many times you encounter people who stop walking by faith and start living by rationale, and God can't perform great things in their lives.

A lack of faith has caused a lot of the church to stumble and die. Anytime a nation becomes blessed and affluent, as described in Deuteronomy 8, God always reminds them: "But thou shalt remember the LORD thy God...." (Deuteronomy 8:18). If it took faith to get you there, it's going to take faith to keep you there. Don't forget Him!

The Bible says in Romans 12:3 "to think soberly, according as God hath dealt to every man the measure of faith." THE measure of faith. There are several interpretations for that but, for this presentation, THE measure of faith means that every person has been given the ability to believe. That's what it means—everyone has THE measure which gives you the ability to believe.

When we were born, we were born equal. You were born with the ability to believe, but what you do with that is highly dependent on how you feed it. Then faith comes how? The Bible says in Romans 10:17, "Faith comes by hearing…" and hearing comes how? "By the word of God…" Faith comes by hearing and hearing comes by the *rhema*.

As you are hearing, you must ask God to help you hear because the way you hear is determined by how you've been shaped. A man came to Jesus who had an afflicted son and asked Jesus to deliver him. In Mark 9:23, 24, this was Jesus' reply: "Jesus said unto him, If thou canst believe, all things are possible to him that believeth. And straightway the father of the child cried out, and said with tears, Lord, I believe; help thou mine unbelief."

Your circumstances can be so overwhelming, the reality so crushing, that it's hard for you to believe. That is the time to draw from THE measure—your ability to believe! Job said in Job 19:25–26: "For I know that my Redeemer lives, and at the last he will stand upon the earth. And after my skin has been thus destroyed, yet in my flesh I shall see God." From that point, Job grows in his faith, until in Job 42:1, he says, "Now I know that You can do everything…." And he did know that because he grew in his faith.

Faith is low in the western church. People don't believe God like they used to. We have people believing God for things and not believing the God of things—we have people who love healing and not the healer. We've given God a shopping list. "Look after my house. God, look after my house. Look after my children, God. God, look after my husband. God, give me a husband. Give me money. Give me clothes. Give me a car. Give me a house." A list of that type doesn't require either relationship with God or faith in God. We need to grow in our faith.

3. **There is a lack of intercessory prayer.** A man once told me, "Pray five minutes a week and you're fine." Five minutes a week? Seven days without prayer makes one weak. W-E-A-K—Seven days without prayer makes one weak. I'm so glad I'm African because God has visited Africa. Africans love to pray. I've been to other places in the world where people haven't prayed in years. I recently visited a large church, and the pastor called for a prayer meeting. Three people came for prayer—three—from a church of thousands.

Following are four facts to help cultivate intercessory prayer:
   a. Prayer must be taught. Luke 11:1 says "Now Jesus was praying in a certain place, and when he finished, one of his disciples said to him, "Lord, teach us to pray, as John taught his disciples."
   b. Prayer must not be an event.
   c. Prayer must be a culture.
   d. Prayer must be who we are, not what we do.

Nations have deteriorated because of the lack of prayer. I was ordained in 1980 on the 8th of November. I was 23 years old. On that Sunday morning, a pastor from the city of Baytown, Texas, near Houston, preached a message using Jeremiah 9 as the text. It was entitled "Where are the Weepers?" He told a story of an event that took place over a twelve-year period from 1929 to 1942. A handful of women wept every day for the United States in their prayer room which was named "The Weeping Willows." They wept and prayed for twelve years. The prayer meeting ended after the United States entered World War II; the revival produced by that prayer meeting ended at the same time. Prayer is the core and the center of what we do. The reason we have so many challenges in our nation is because there's a lack of prayer.

Since the system took prayer out of schools in America and in different countries in the Western Civilization, including in Africa, we've seen decadence creeping into the lives of our children because the spiritual center has been corroded. Teach your children how to pray. Pray with them and let them see and hear you pray.

You also need to pray with your congregation and let them hear you pray. Recently, a respected leader and close friend of the ministry shared a story with our leaders that rocked me to the core. One Sunday during a service as the Holy Spirit was moving, he said that he went to the altar and knelt. He was weeping and praying and when he eventually got up, some of the guys in the church were waiting for him. Several of them had been raised in the church and one (a teenager) said to him, "Bishop, I've been here all my life and that's the first time I've seen you praying at the altar." The young man said, "I want you to teach me. Teach me to pray." Our churches need to see us pray.

In the many places I travel—105 different conferences and meetings this year—I can tell you, there's very little prayer. There's no power or anointing where there's no prayer. When ChiChi and I travel to the United States, we host prayer meetings and prayer summits, and people come from everywhere because they want to know how to pray. It is disheartening to realize that the fundamental component of our Christian faith, prayer—the means by which we have relationship with God—is not being taught and, worse yet, not being modeled within the body of Christ!

4. **There's a lack of worship.** I know we're busy. I know that we've got to do another service. I know that some churches have more than one service going on. There's one excuse after another, but

that doesn't negate the fact that there is a lack of worship. I've been to places where they turn the sound system down; if you start shouting, they shut you down and you're not even allowed to say "amen" in church. The expression of worship is very, very limited. One argument against extravagant worship is that you cannot equate emotionalism and culture to worship. Yet the Bible is clear; it says in Psalm 47:1, "Clap your hands, all you peoples! Shout to God with a voice of triumph!" You can't shout without being emotional! You can't clap your hands without being emotional.

There are seven different Hebrew words for worship, and each one uses a type of demonstration—Barak, Halal, Shachah, Tehillah, Todah, Yadah, and Zamar. Each one has an emotion involved with the demonstration. Worship in many of today's churches has been eroded and stripped down to a religious practice, void of its original purpose which was to glorify and praise God. Do we practice "entering His gates with thanksgiving and His courts with praise…" as we read in Psalm 100:4?

We wonder why we're in trouble, and we wonder why there's a deficit. The devil is intent on discarding worship in our churches and worship in our personal lives because the Bible says in Psalm 22:3, "He [God] inhabits the praises of Israel." So the less praise, the less God inhabits. The Bible says in Psalm 149:6–9, "Let the high praises of God be in their mouth, and a two-edged sword in their hand; To execute vengeance upon the heathen, and punishments upon the people; To bind their kings with chains, and their nobles with fetters of iron; To execute upon them the judgment written: this honour have all his saints. Praise ye the LORD." When we offer high praise we actually are binding kings and nobles and demonic princes with chains. The devil has tried to take worship out because he doesn't want to be bound.

But here's the thing—you watch a game when Newcastle is playing Chelsea, and it's at St. James Stadium in northeast

England. Those guys come out in their black and white stripes having one of the best days of the season, and then they score a goal. Do you know what it sounds like when 60,000 Geordies in that stadium begin to shout and scream?

I've also watched American football on television when the Green Bay Packers are playing in their hometown in Wisconsin in the northern part of the U. S. Many times that team will play in sub-zero weather; but watch what the fans do. You'll see guys in the stands with their shirts off, painted green and wearing cheese hats, screaming and shouting in freezing cold sub-zero weather for their team. The same thing happens at any other sports event. There's shouting and screaming and worshipping! But then you take the same men and women and put them in church, and suddenly they turn into monks. They are meek little people without energy or passion.

We need to bring the passion and energy into our churches. We MUST bless the Lord at all times. I WILL demonstrate my worship. It's important that we bring worship back with power and passion. Thank God for songwriters like Israel Houghton who have brought the presence of God back into our worship. He's a melodist. He's a lyricist. He adds all those components and makes the sum total worship experience available to a person.

I want to take a moment to address all praise and worship leaders and songwriters: Don't write bubble gum songs. Write inspiring songs that are authentic and activate the spirit of a man to honor and co-labor with the Spirit of God. The reason we have challenges is because worship has been taken out of churches. I will worship Him; at ALL times I will bless Him.

5. **Problems emerge from a lack of understanding the times**.
1 Chronicles tells us that there was a certain one of the tribes of Israel who had understanding of the times. It was the tribe

of Issachar. 1 Chronicles 12:32 says, "And of the children of Issachar, which were men that had understanding of the times, to know what Israel ought to do; the heads of them were two hundred; and all their brethren were at their commandment." They had an anointing to understand the times and because of that understanding, they knew what to do and when to do it.

Jesus addressed this issue in Matthew 16:1–3.

> *"The Pharisees also with the Sadducees came, and tempting desired him that he would shew them a sign from heaven. He answered and said unto them, When it is evening, ye say, It will be fair weather: for the sky is red. And in the morning, It will be foul weather today: for the sky is red and lowering. O ye hypocrites, ye can discern the face of the sky; but can ye not discern the signs of the times?"*

They missed the day of their visitation. We must understand where we are because when we understand the times, we can maximize what God is doing in a place. When it's your time, and you don't understand it, you miss an opportunity of a lifetime.

Politicians may feel they are supposed to be government leaders, but if they don't recognize the right timing and put together a solid campaign, people aren't going to vote for them. We must do more than recognize our gifts, talents, and callings; we must understand the seasons in which they are to be employed. We must prepare for our "hour of visitation" and maximize what we have been given by doing our part to prepare ourselves.

A church is the same way. If we in the church don't recognize times and seasons, we'll be plowing when it's time to harvest, or trying to harvest when it's time to plow. Instead of walking down to greet our groom, we'll be in the barn milking a cow. Rather than attending a celebration, we'll be asleep under a tree. If we are not aware of the seasons in our lives, we can miss our opportunity, and sadly some opportunities come only once in a lifetime.

In 1985, the Lord opened a door for me to see a different world at the Reinhardt Bonnke Fire Conference. I began to see a world of Christianity, a world of Pentecostalism, and the Charismatic Movement in a very significant way. When I saw that world at the International Conference Center in Harare, I also saw some of what I was going to become in the future, both locally and internationally.

When that happened, I began to recognize that God was opening doors for the future; so I then had to start making preparation. I had a little inkling that God was sending me to preach to African Americans, so I began to study their culture. I began to watch Roots and read books like Malcolm X and Mohammed Ali's life story in order to familiarize myself with their culture. I also began to study and observe different preaching styles. From that time, it took 10 years for a door to open. I only had one chance, just one.

As the years went by, I invited another young pastor to a platform that I had built. I said to this person, "Now that you're coming on this platform, this is what you must do because you're only going to get one chance, one chance." Very influential pastors, teachers, and worship leaders were in that meeting. This person was given the opening night of the conference, and I told him exactly what to do. He only had one chance.

That night, he came in with a pair of red Nike shoes that were so bright. I thought, "What in the world is this?" He wore a suit with red Nike shoes at a major conference so, as he walked on the stage, I could already see people shaking their heads. Instead of maximizing that moment, he chose shoes that caused the people to write him off. He chose a difficult subject, perhaps to show off, but after 20 minutes, he broke down on that major international conference scene. I tried to pick up the pieces but it just didn't work. In my opinion that individual, who is more talented than I am, missed an opportunity of a lifetime. Many of the doors that have opened for me would have opened for him; and he would have gone further than I would have. When people don't recognize their time, problems emerge.

My prayer for you, dear reader, is that God grant you wisdom to understand the times and the season. I pray that you will maximize your moment, preparing today for what the future holds. I pray that you will use your God-given gifts and talents to further the Kingdom of God and that you will witness a bold and undeniable increase of His Kingdom in your life and in the lives of those around you.

SECTION TWO
KINGDOM INCREASE

INCREASE OF THE KINGDOM

CHAPTER 5
KINGDOMS, DIMENSIONS & LAWS

In section one, we addressed the issues that often arise that prevent the increase that comes with the Kingdom of God. In this section, we will discuss the dynamics of Kingdom Increase, beginning first with a brief review of what was mentioned in the overview within the first chapter of this book, then moving into the meat of chapter six which involves types of kingdoms and the dimensions and laws within kingdoms.

As stated in the introduction of this book, I believe that a generation will arise in the earth realm which will be built on a solid foundation of Biblical revelation. Once that solid foundation is built, the truth will be revealed, and the truth will set us free. Once that truth is revealed, satan and his bottomless pit systems will be displaced. This overcoming generation will unleash in the earth a system that will last for a millennium, a thousand years.

In the introduction, I listed the following ten "truths" concerning the way the Kingdom of God functions:

1. The nature of the Kingdom is increase.
2. The dynamics of the Kingdom is everything gets better.
3. The power of the Kingdom is force.
4. The culture of the Kingdom is service. You cannot get what is rightfully yours until you've served someone or something.
5. The order of the Kingdom is structure.
6. The anointing of the Kingdom is gifts.

7. The success of the Kingdom is generational dominion.
8. The currency of the Kingdom is faith.
9. The strength of the Kingdom is unity. Agreement is the strength of the Kingdom.
10. The access to the Kingdom is through understanding mysteries.

Isaiah 9:7 is foundational for understanding Kingdom Increase: "And of the increase of his government and peace, there shall be no end." A generation is coming that will establish His government and His peace. There are foundational systems within the kingdom that are the basis for its structure. Within the structure of the Kingdom of God, Jesus, tells us in Matthew 6:33 to "…seek ye first the kingdom of God, and his righteousness; and all these things shall be added unto you."

Classifications of Kingdoms

The highest of all the kingdoms is the Kingdom of God. "Seek first the Kingdom of God," tells us that, if there's a first kingdom, there have to be other kingdoms. There are seven kingdoms which are part of the earthly realm:

1. The Kingdom of God

2. The angelic kingdom—The angelic kingdom is divided into two parts:
   a) Angels that have remained in the Kingdom of Light with God.
   b) Angels that have fallen to their low estate as described in Jude 1:6: "And the angels which kept not their first estate, but left their own habitation, he hath reserved in everlasting chains under darkness unto the judgment of the great day." This is Lucifer and the angels that went with him. Revelation 12:7–11 describes the battle that took place when that happened—"And there was war in heaven: Michael and his angels fought against the dragon; and the dragon fought and his angels, And prevailed not; neither was their place found any more in heaven. And the great dragon was cast out, that

old serpent, called the Devil, and Satan, which deceiveth the whole world: he was cast out into the earth, and his angels were cast out with him."

One third of the angels went with him, so the devil set up his kingdom in the earth. In Matthew 12:25–30, Jesus recognized the satanic kingdom: "And if Satan cast out Satan, he is divided against himself; how shall then his kingdom stand?" Satan is the head of his kingdom of fallen angels.

3. The planetary kingdom or the kingdom of the celestials— The Bible talks about this in 1 Corinthians 15:40. "There are also celestial bodies, and bodies terrestrial: but the glory of the celestial is one, and the glory of the terrestrial is another." There are various planets and celestial bodies which are in the stratosphere of the various heavens.

4. The kingdom of man—Daniel 4:17 tells us, "The sentence is by the decree of the watchers, the decision by the word of the holy ones, to the end that the living may know that the Most High rules the kingdom of men and gives it to whom he will and sets over it the lowliest of men." (ESV).God sets up the most unlikely people in the kingdom of man.

5. The animal kingdom
6. The kingdom of vegetation and plants
7. The mineral kingdom which is divided into three parts

Within the structures of these kingdoms, there are orders and protocols that must be understood. Once we understand these orders and protocols, we can gain access to them. The way we access these kingdoms is through the gift of revelation knowledge.

Seek First the Kingdom
When we look to God to establish His Kingdom in the earth, we expect

God's nature to be released in the earth. In the Garden of Eden, Adam was created in God's image and God's likeness. Adam had a mind that was in touch with the mind of God. When the Bible says in Philippians 2:5, "Let this mind which was in Christ Jesus be in you," the word Christ means "anointed one." The mind of Christ was the mind of Adam. Adam was the anointed one in the earth. That mind was fully aware of everything that was happening both in heaven and in earth. The Bible says that God would speak with Adam every day, in the cool of the day. According to Genesis 1:5, the Bible counts a day, not from morning to evening but from the evening to the morning: "And God called the light Day, and the darkness he called Night. And the evening and the morning were the first day."

The evening to the morning was the first day; so when God would come to Adam in the evening, He would come at the beginning of the new day. That time frame defines the structure of the new day coming; God would then share His thoughts, which are higher thoughts, and His ways, which are higher ways according to Isaiah 55:9. He would share those thoughts with His son, Adam. Then, Adam, in the new day would begin to implement what God was saying in the earth.

I want you to understand the importance of the way the Kingdom works. The Bible says in Genesis 1:14 that on the fourth day of creation, God made the sun, the moon, and the stars—the sun to rule the day, the moon to rule the night. Then God made the stars as the crowning glory of that creation. The sun represents apostolic leadership.

When Joseph had a dream, he saw the sun, the moon and the stars, and he told his dad, Jacob, about this dream.

> Then he dreamed another dream and told it to his brothers
> and said, "Behold, I have dreamed another dream.
> Behold, the sun, the moon, and eleven stars were bowing
> down to me." But when he told it to his father and to his
> brothers, his father rebuked him and said to him, "What

*is this dream that you have dreamed? Shall I and your
mother and your brothers indeed come to bow ourselves
to the ground before you?"* Genesis 37:9–10 ESV

When you see the sun in Genesis 1:14–18, God is revealing that an
apostolic order has been established in the earth. That apostolic order
is to establish the Kingdom of God. "And God made two great lights;
the greater light to rule the day, and the lesser light to rule the night: he
made the stars also." So the sun, then, rules the day.

The sun is the revelation knowledge that comes into the earth that defines
the day. So when David says in Psalm 118:24, "This is the day that the
Lord has made; we will rejoice and be glad in it," he was saying, "The
sun will rule the day." There is a key revelation that rules a day. It's a
key revelation, a thought, an idea, that rules a day. David said in Psalm
90:4, "For a thousand years in thy sight are but as yesterday when it is
past, and as a watch in the night."

When you see the reference to a thousand years in Revelation 20:2,
it means there is a day that's coming; and that day is defined by a
revelation, an apostolic order that's set in the earth: "And he laid hold
on the dragon, that old serpent, which is the Devil, and Satan, and bound
him a thousand years, And cast him into the bottomless pit, and shut
him up, and set a seal upon him, that he should deceive the nations no
more, till the thousand years should be fulfilled: and after that he must
be loosed a little season." The revelation defines the day.

The revelation of the day is the Kingdom of God established in
dominion. The Kingdom of God, however, cannot be established in
the natural mind. It has to be established in the renewed mind. Paul
writes to the church in Romans 12:2, "And be not conformed to this
world: but be ye transformed by the renewing of your mind, that ye
may prove what is that good, and acceptable, and perfect, will of God."
He says very implicitly that we must not be conformed to this world.
Why? Because it is built on a bottomless pit. It's built on sand; it's

built on a system that is foundationless. But we must be transformed by renewing our minds that we might prove what is that good, acceptable, and perfect will of God.

Dimensions

The good, acceptable, and perfect will of God is laid out in three distinct dimensions. Let's compare those three dimensions to Moses' Tabernacle which was constructed while the children of Israel wandered in the desert.

The good will of God is like the courtyard where the common people were allowed to congregate. The acceptable will of God is the Holy Place or outer chamber, allowing access to the priestly tribe. The perfect will of God represents the Holiest of Holies which housed the Ark of the Covenant, and only the High Priest could enter.

Let's examine how we can live in the dimensions of God's good, acceptable, and perfect will:

1. The good will of God refers to the flesh or the body. This is compared to entering the courtyard of the tabernacle. Ephesians 5:18 says, "Speaking to yourselves in psalms and hymns and spiritual songs, singing and making melody in your heart to the Lord." Psalms are for the flesh and inspire the body to worship God. Psalm 34:1 says, "I will bless the Lord at all times." How does the body worship God? With clapping of hands, with shouting, with dancing. That's God's good will.

2. The acceptable will of God is the soulish realm where we relate to the Lord from our soul. Entering the Holy Place brings us to the next level of worship. We find God's acceptable will when "My SOUL doth magnify the Lord," as Mary said in Luke 1:46. Your soul is the seat of your will and your emotions. Worship that employs your will and emotions places you in God's acceptable will.

3. The perfect will of God is when we walk in the spirit. It's then that we enter into the Holy of Holies and encounter Him in Spirit. Galatians 5:16 says, "This I say then, Walk in the Spirit, and ye shall not fulfil the lust of the flesh." God desires for us to be in the Spirit. He wants us to be in His perfect will in which our body and soul aligns with the Spirit.

In 1 Corinthians 14:13, Paul says, "What is it then? I will pray with the spirit, and I will pray with the understanding also: I will sing with the spirit, and I will sing with the understanding also." If people worship and only have a physical demonstration, they find God's good will. If we get into the soulish realm, involving our will and emotions, we are in God's acceptable will; but our goal should be to find God's perfect will, being one with His Spirit.

God's perfect will is that we align ourselves in spirit according to what God does, but that cannot happen until the mind is renewed. The mind has to be renewed; it has to go back to its original state. I'm not speaking in terms of intellect or academic ability because that wouldn't be possible. Everyone is different. If every person's mind was renewed according to intellect or academic ability, every person in the whole world with a renewed mind would have the same abilities. Our mind must be renewed regarding our perception of the Kingdom and the will of God in the earth. What is the will of God in the earth, for you, for me, for the purpose of God in the earth? Everyone has a different IQ. That is your quotient of intelligence release. When he says that our mind must be renewed, Paul is not talking about everyone having an IQ above 180, which is genius. Adam was an academic genius, but the truth is, Eve was not on the same academic level as Adam. She was beguiled (manipulated and deceived) by that serpent in the garden. If she were at the same academic level as Adam, she would have been able to respond the same way Adam responded when he was tested and tempted. The point here is that every human being, regardless of our level of gifting or intelligence, must align ourselves in our minds, to fulfill the perfect will of God. We must align ourselves with Kingdom mentality.

Romans 14:17 tells us, "For the kingdom of God is not meat and drink; but righteousness, and peace, and joy in the Holy Ghost." That's the Kingdom of God—righteousness, peace and joy IN the Holy Ghost. Righteousness is God's standard in the earth. Peace is God's comfort in the earth. And joy is His strength in the earth: "The joy of the Lord is our strength." Nehemiah 8:10. The joy of the Lord is having comfort in what God has given you. You can have someone who has gained a lot wealth living in a nice house but is unhappy. You can have someone that's living in a mud hut and ironing on the floor who is so comforted, so happy because they understand the joy of the Lord. That's what gives us strength.

When we begin to release the Kingdom of God within the earth realm, it's because we are all coming into alignment with what God is saying. Alignment brings apostolic order. When God establishes an apostolic leader, we have an apostolic house, and all the gifts align themselves to that order. Apostolic alignment is how the Kingdom is released in the earth. According to Romans 12:4–5, we are all members of the same body: "For as in one body we have many members, and the members do not all have the same function, so we, though many, are one body in Christ, and individually members one of another."

Christ is the head of that body; so as a body, we align ourselves accordingly. The apostle John, who wrote in the book of Revelation to the seven churches in Asia Minor, spoke to each of the churches, beginning in Ephesus and ending with the church of Laodicea. Each letter is addressed to the angel of the church of Ephesus, Smyrna, Pergamos, etc. He named each of the churches, but the letter is actually addressed to the angel or the apostolic leader. Everyone in that church grouping is formulated under apostolic order and apostolic alignment. The same is true with each of the churches that Paul visited. There is apostolic alignment in Antioch, then again in Damascus which was under the apostolic leadership of Ananias. When he started the church in Ephesus, Priscilla and Acquilla were in leadership, creating apostolic alignment. According to Acts 20:4, men like Secundus, Tychicus, and Trophimus, who were all leading different churches, accompanied

Paul, who was the chief apostle: "And there accompanied him into Asia Sopater of Berea; and of the Thessalonians, Aristarchus and Secundus; and Gaius of Derbe, and Timotheus; and of Asia, Tychicus and Trophimus."

The Kingdom of God is released in the earth through apostolic government and apostolic oversight with everyone coming under that alignment. It is the apostles who reveal the will of God in the earth. Once they reveal that will in apostolic alignment, we are going to see the increase of the Kingdom of God.

The Bible says this in Hebrews 3:1–2 ESV: "Therefore, holy brothers, you who share in a heavenly calling, consider Jesus, the apostle and high priest of our confession, who was faithful to him who appointed him, just as Moses also was faithful in all God's house."

Jesus is the Chief Apostle. Paul continued by saying that Moses in his day built the house, but Jesus IS the house. Moses served the house but Jesus is the One that established the house. Because Jesus is the Chief Apostle, we align under His teaching and principles.

The Kingdom of God can only be ingrained in our hearts when our minds are renewed to understand apostolic alignment. When we understand apostolic alignment, we then prove what is that good will, which are the works of our bodies. Do not allow the root of bitterness to contaminate your soul because then you violate God's acceptable will. Finally, do not quench the Spirit because then you violate God's perfect will. The Kingdom of God is activated and released in our lives when we align ourselves with God's will.

Let's talk now about increase—the nature of the Kingdom is increase. Increase is built into the system. When you study the dynamics of God's world, the Kingdom world, everything starts with a seed. Everything, human beings included, starts with a seed. There are many things we can say about the seed, but one of the things a seed does is change a cycle. Every mother knows that a seed will change a cycle. A seed begins to prepare for a harvest in the future.

Every seed comes as one, single seed. Every seed has several components in it. The more dynamic the components of the seed, the more dynamic is the harvest. When a seed from a male is sowed into a female, whether it's in the animal world or in the world of human beings, that seed carries within it the dynamics of tremendous increase. It's interesting to think that a man, a big, tall man, at some point in his journey, was a microscopic seed. But increase is built into the system. When we begin to understand the dynamics of the Kingdom of God, we can expect increase.

Galatians 6: 7, 8 tells us, "Be not deceived; God is not mocked: for whatsoever a man soweth, that shall he also reap. For he that soweth to his flesh shall of the flesh reap corruption; but he that soweth to the Spirit shall of the Spirit reap life everlasting." You can see how that truth actually works in two ways—When you sow a seed of bitterness or hate, increase is built into the system. Genesis 8:22 says, "as long as the earth remaineth, seedtime and harvest…shall not cease." The devil understands this principle more than human beings understand it, so the devil's entire function is to keep our minds degenerate to insure that we sow the wrong seeds.

Let's go back and look at the original sin. The Bible says in Romans 5:12, "…through one man sin entered the world….," so we see it's the man that brought sin into the world, not the woman. The woman was deceived, but Adam, through an act of his will, allowed sin to enter. Eve didn't say in her mind, "I'm going to eat this fruit; I'm making up my mind to eat this fruit;" she was deceived into doing it. Adam, however, made a decision; he chose. His choice was a seed; and he sowed an act of disobedience. Therefore, Adam then had to reap the fruit of disobedience. The Bible says in Romans 6:23, "For the wages of sin is death." You receive wages for your work, so when Adam chose to disobey, his mind worked, and it got paid.

If the wages of sin is death, the wages of righteousness is life. 2 Corinthians 5:21 ESV tells us, "For our sake he made him to be sin who knew no sin, so that in him we might become the righteousness of God." Jesus chose to be righteous. He came to earth, and through an act of His will chose to die, saying in Matthew 26:39, "O my Father, if it be possible, let this cup pass from me: nevertheless not as I will, but as thou wilt." He said in John 10:18a, "No one takes it [my life] from me, but I lay it down of my own accord." When He was buried as a sinner, he wasn't paid as a sinner; He was paid for righteousness. He rose from the dead because the wages of righteousness is life. The Kingdom of God is where we choose righteousness, peace, and joy. Righteousness is God's standard in the earth. It was an act of Adam's will that ushered in the wages of death. It was an act of Jesus' will that now brings the wages of righteousness and life. We now have a choice to choose either life or death.

Everything in life is a seed—everything. Reading this book, attending seminars, listening to radio or CD teachings are all seeds being sown. The principles in this book are seeds being sown, seeds that may produce a tremendous harvest for decades, even centuries to come! We must not underestimate the power of the seed and its potential for influence.

All revelation and all truth is past, present, and future. The other day, I found a teaching by Derek Prince from 1978. It's past, but I heard it yesterday which made the truth present, and when I share it with you, it's going to be future. All revelation is past, present, and future. What you're hearing now is not new; it's already been said at one time or another. The reason we say it again is because there's the future; there's a generation that still needs to hear it.

Jesus lived 2,000 years ago; that's the past. In revival services, though, somebody's going to give his heart to the Lord; and he'll become acquainted with Jesus in the present. When we're dealing with the dynamics of the Kingdom of God, we have to understand that anytime a seed is sown, it's for the past; it's for the present; it's for the future. That seed will change the cycle of your life, and it will produce a different harvest for your life.

If you're living your life in a way that you are earning the wages of death, you can begin to sow the seed of righteousness. As long as there remains seedtime and harvest, the righteous seed you have sown will overrule the death cycle that has been paying you. The dynamics of the Kingdom is increase.

What God requires us to do on the first level of the Kingdom is to begin to sow the kinds of seeds that cancel demonic stupidity and nonsense. Every day you sow a seed of goodness. Every day you sow a seed of kindness. At the beginning of this year, I gave two offerings. The first one was our tithe which the Lord inspired me to pay a year in advance. And the second offering was $365. I wanted to make certain that I put a dollar seed in the ground for every day of the year because if I sow every day, I will reap every day. "Whatsoever a man soweth that also shall he reap." If I sow a dollar a day, I'm getting a harvest for every day. So every day, I expect to receive something.

When you make a sacrifice in an area of lack in your life and sow a seed, you will reverse the cycle. For example, save money on gasoline by walking when you can, and sow those savings into the Kingdom. Fast an occasional meal, and give your savings to someone in need. Deny yourself in order to sow good seed. The devil hates that, because you can reverse the cycle of poverty and lack when you sow good seed. That's why you must sow a seed in every area of your life.

Every year, I give away clothes, computers, motor vehicles, and tickets; every year I give money for scholarships and help people because I want that harvest. We have sown money into other people's building programs. This year we bought wonderful sound systems for two different churches because the sound system in our new church is going to cost a million dollars. The video equipment and cameras will also cost close to a million dollars. We can't afford that now, but if we sow a seed, the harvest will come back.

Let me give you an example of how that COULD happen. Let's say there's a little church over here that needs a couple of video cameras so we will give them those video cameras. When the new cathedral is built, a company like Sony could come into the region and say, "This is an incredible building; it's a landmark building; it's a building that literally will be counted as one of the seven wonders of Zimbabwe so let's get on the bandwagon; let's give them the television equipment they need." We sow seeds knowing that God is Lord of the harvest, and He can make impossible things possible.

Consider where you are right now—you may be struggling to pay for your night school. You've got small kids, so you're going to sow seeds and put somebody's kid through school because 18–20 years from now, when your son goes to Harvard or to the University of London, somebody from the next generation or a wealthy institution will pay your child's entire scholarship and tuition in full. How will it happen? Through the principle of seed, time, and harvest.

Laws

When the devil took over from Adam, he imposed the culture from his kingdom on humanity. When Jesus came on the scene, He said, "… My kingdom is not of this world…" Jesus came to impose the culture of heaven on this world. The culture of heaven is generosity. That's the reason we give—God is generous. He doesn't give you just one; He gives you everything.

A human being is grown from one seed, one sperm; but millions of sperm are released in order for one to be planted. If every sperm made connection, all of the African population could be produced! The point is that God works in multiplicity—He produces millions of sperm through just one act. He could have just put one seed in a woman to produce one child, but instead he chose to release millions of seeds. God is a generous God. So God has come to impose in the earth His nature through Jesus Christ. Harvest and multiplication are built into the system of Increase. When we're dealing with the dynamics of harvest, there are a number of laws that we have to apply and consider. Three of these laws are listed below:

1. **The Law of Kinds**—In the Law of Kinds, everything produces after its kind. If you want a certain kind, you have to plant that particular seed. Usually I can tell what kind a person is by the people they hang around with. Examine the aspects that are part of your life—the people, priorities, the values, etc. If you don't like the kind of things you are producing, you have to sow the kind of seed you want to grow.

   What kind of a husband or wife do you want? What kind of a family do you want? What kind of a church do you want? What kind of worship do you want? What kind of a nation do you want? What kind of leaders do you want? You sow the kind you want, and you reap the kind you want. It's the Law of Kinds.

2. **The Law of Diversity**—God didn't make one species of a thing. He could have just made Jersey cows or He could have just made Brahman cows; but there are dozens of species of cows. Did you know there are 147 different species of bees in a certain sector in the United Kingdom? The same is true of most animals in the animal kingdom. When you are sowing in kind, you have to also diversify your sowing. Sow your gift, your time, and your knowledge to reap a harvest in the Kingdom. Duplicate God's law and diversify your sowing.

3. **The Law of Logic and Rationale**—The Law of Logic and Rationale simply means that if it's true here, then it's true over there. Let me explain using this example: I'm holding a bottle of water. It's water in Zimbabwe. When I go to Nigeria next week

and I take this with me, it doesn't change into something else because it's in Nigeria. It's still water in Nigeria, H_2O, because if it's true over here, then it's true over there.

In other words, if Abraham did this and it's true for Abraham, then it's true for me here. If it's true for Creflo Dollar over there, then it's true for Tudor Bismark over here. It's the Law of Logic and Rationale. Acts 10:34 says, "…God is no respecter of persons." God honors those who honor and implement principles.

In the Law of Logic and Rationale, you can say, "If I sow in a famine, I will reap a harvest." If I sow a tomato, I will not be surprised when I reap a tomato. But the devil and the system of the demonic world will try to deceive you. He will plant lies in your mind regarding the good seed you sow and tell you it's not worth it. You must refute that lie and declare, "I sowed a good seed and I'm expecting that harvest."

When we understand that logic and rationale are built into the system and we sow our seed in faith, that seed is going to produce at some point in the future because the harvest is built into the system. Every woman that has a baby from a seed that is sown has confidence in her life and heart that, when she gives birth, she will give birth to a little human being, not to a lizard… or a rat. It's the Law of Logic and Rationale.

Multiplication

The dynamics of the Kingdom is increase—it's built into the system. The other component of increase is **multiplication**. God always promises that He will multiply you. The word ply is level or layer. Plywood is an example—it means wood that is layered. When you buy tires you can either by 4-ply or 8-ply; that's eight little grooves in the tire—eight layers. The more the layers, the greater is the grip; the more the layers, the stronger is the wood.

When God says, "I will multiply you," He actually is telling you, "I will multi-layer you." If you have one ply, and the devil comes with a karate chop, he can snap you. But after you've been living your life in righteousness for a while and God multi-plies you, I don't care what kind of bazooka the devil throws at you, he'll never be able to break you because you are multi-layered. That's why God wants you to sow so that He can multi-level or multi-layer your finance. That's why God wants you to give your tithes so that your generations can be multi-layered. Evil in the world today is multi-plying. The things teenagers go through today as opposed to what we went through as teenagers 40 years ago are two completely different things in terms of temptation, sexual stuff, drugs, and so on—it's two different worlds.

When I was 17 and first started preaching 39 years ago, I was taught to pay my tithes. My tithe was creating multi-levels/multi-layers of protection for my life because evil is multiplying. My seed is going to now shield my children and my children's children from what's coming. When Abraham paid his tithes, he was building layers for his children to survive the worst slavery the world had ever seen. Abraham's children survived 400 years of Egyptian slavery for one reason. Abraham built multi-ply-cation.

If you think evil is tough now, 20 years from now, it's going to be so frightening to see the ways evil will increase. ChiChi and I have certain places in the world we want to visit, so we travelled to the city of New Orleans. I've always wanted to go to New Orleans because growing up I played in a jazz band. We played different jazz pieces, many of them from Louisiana and New Orleans, so my desire was to go to Bourbon Street which you could call the epicenter for jazz.

When we got to the entrance of Bourbon Street, there was a young black jazz band playing. There were trumpets and trombones; it was a horn jazz band, and it was incredible. I thought, "This is it! My dream has come true. This is one of the things I've always planned for my life."

But as we stepped INTO Bourbon Street, off the top of my head, I can't tell you of any other place in the world that's more evil. It's one of the very few places in the world where I felt demonic spirits actually sticking on me, even licking me! While we were walking down the street, there were women wearing garlands around their necks. Each garland they were wearing represented the number of times the woman had shown her breasts to the public. During certain times of the year, it is reported that even public sexual acts are performed during the gay parades and Mardi Gras. We wouldn't even eat at the restaurants there on Bourbon Street. We went to another street and vowed we'd never go back because of the evil there. Evil there is multi-plied; and it is multi-plying in other locations as well.

Once we have a generation that understands that increase is in the system, that generation will sow seeds in the present that will shield our future generations.

CHAPTER 6
PROGRESS, FORCE & SERVICE

The dynamics of the Kingdom is that everything gets better. The Bible says in Psalm 30:5 that "weeping endures for a night, but joy comes in the morning." In our world, we have to endure seasons; we have to endure days, years, and certain patterns.

When a female baby is born, everything that is needed for life is built into her the day she's born. But a year later, that female cannot have a baby of her own because even though she has every component needed to be a female, there are certain things that are not developed in that female's physical body. She will then enter a season at some point in her life where she will be able to bear children. Then, as the years and the seasons go by, those functions stop functioning in the same manner. But that doesn't mean that a woman who's 80 years old and a baby that's eight weeks old are not females. It just means that they are in different seasons and cycles in their lives.

We have to understand that in whatever season or cycle of our life that we are, the dynamics of the kingdom is that everything gets better. Everything gets better. Let's look at the principle of advantages and disadvantages.

To everything there are advantages and disadvantages. I'll give you a couple of quick examples. There's an advantage to being single, but there's also a disadvantage to being single. Some of you just want to get married; and there are advantages to getting married; there are also disadvantages to getting married. If you're a guy, you have a "wifey" now, so there's someone else besides yourself to consider any time there's a decision to make. And you women have a husband, so you have responsibilities you didn't have before.

There are advantages to having a job and working, and there are disadvantages to having a job and working. The advantage to working is that you will get paid and have all those wonderful things; but then, there are disadvantages because people who are working can't just pick up and go wherever they want, anytime they want. The same is true of being a parent. There are advantages to being a parent, but there are also disadvantages. When you are a young couple, you can spend a night on the town, or say, "Let's go to all-night prayer!" Now that you're a mother, you can't go to all-night prayer. You've got a baby that needs mommy.

There are advantages to being old—wisdom is one. But there are also advantages to being young. We've got the Tudor Bismark 10K Run coming up soon; in the last six months, I've been struggling to try to keep my 10K's on 55 minutes. Last year, it was easy. This year, it's difficult.

There are advantages to everything, and there are disadvantages to everything. You have to learn in the Kingdom of God to work with both. Being in a storm has its disadvantages—the chaos, the difficulty, the uncertainty. It also has its advantages—the rain, the temperature change, the new perspective it brings. Every challenge brings new wisdom when it is approached with a teachable spirit.

We must look for the benefits in any situation, the silver lining within every cloud. We must believe the Word when it tells us "all things work together for good to them that love God, to them who are the called according to his purpose." (Romans 8:28) If we love God and are called according to His purpose, we must know the end is good. The outcome will be good, even if the present circumstance is bad. In the Kingdom, everything gets better. Period. It doesn't get worse, nor does it stay the same. It marches forward, upward; it never goes backward. It never lessens. The dynamic of the Kingdom is that everything always gets better.

Let's go to the book of Job. Job 42 tells us the end of Job's horrendous trial. It is here in this trial and test that Job discovers God; secondly, Job discovers himself; and thirdly, Job discovers his friends. Job 42:1 says, "Then Job replied to the LORD: "I know that you can do all things; no purpose of yours can be thwarted." Through the experience of losing everything, he found out this truth—the Lord can do everything.

In Job 42:10–12 ESV, we see turnaround:

> "After Job had prayed for his friends, the LORD restored
> his fortunes and gave him twice as much as he had
> before. All his brothers and sisters and everyone who had
> known him before came and ate with him in his house.
> They comforted and consoled him over all the trouble the
> LORD had brought on him, and each one gave him a piece
> of silver and a gold ring. The LORD blessed the latter part
> of Job's life more than the former part."

The Lord restored Job when he prayed for his friends; and the Lord gave Job twice as much as he had before. The Bible goes on to say that all his brothers and sisters and all who had been his acquaintance before came to have something to eat with him. They bemoaned him and comforted him over all the evil that the Lord had brought upon him; every man gave him some money and everybody gave him some gold. Now look at verse 12a—"So the LORD blessed the latter end of Job more than his beginning." The latter end was more blessed than the beginning.

Let's take a closer look at verse 11, telling us about Job's brothers and sisters. I didn't even know until I read this closely that Job had brothers and sisters. If you read Chapter 1 in Job, the Bible just tells you about Job and his children. My personal opinion is that Job's trial was connected to his siblings. They were not prospering the way he was, so his calamity and devastation and his eventual reinstatement and elevation were necessary in order for his brothers and sisters to be drawn to him.

Now watch this: The Bible says here that even friends he had been acquainted with weren't following the principles of Job. They came to comfort him; every man gave him a piece of money; and everyone gave him an earring of gold. In other words, they gave him gold, and they gave him a piece of money. The thought there is, "We are sowing into what God has done in your life," because we want what God has done for you.

In Chapter 1, they didn't want to have anything to do with Job; they weren't acquainted with Job's stuff. Now, when they see that God has blessed him, they want a part of it. Do you remember how the devil came to the Lord at a council meeting? "Now there was a day when the sons of God came to present themselves before the LORD, and Satan came also among them. And the LORD said unto Satan, Hast thou considered my servant Job, that there is none like him in the earth, a perfect and an upright man, one that feareth God, and escheweth evil?" (Job 1: 6, 8) God had no other servants like Job—none in all the earth. This trial that he endured produced more servants of the Lord, including Job's family and friends. Now the devil had to consider all those added as the Lord's servants.

So if you're going through something, remember it's not just about you. God is using your 'something' to bring your brothers or sisters or your family members to walk in the path that you have chosen. When they are converted, the devil will go to the next council meeting, and God will say, "Have you considered my servants, Tudor, my sister Bernie, Donovan, Clyde, etc." because, before the trial, they were not in the prosperity environment. After trial, after my elevation, they are now convinced.

Job didn't need his friends' money, but the Bible says, however, that his brothers and sisters, every man, gave him a piece of money. Job didn't need their money. His life had been devastated, and money was not what he needed. Nevertheless, they needed to sow into his life. They were giving into his kind. And then when they did that, God made the end of Job better than his beginning because in the dynamics of the Kingdom, everything gets better. It gets better!

If today is tough, live it anyway; tomorrow is going to be better. If the storm is overwhelming, face it anyway; it won't last forever. Know that things will get better if you are a member of God's Kingdom. Everything goes from faith to faith and glory to glory: "But we all, with open face beholding as in a glass the glory of the Lord, are changed into the same image from glory to glory, even as by the Spirit of the Lord" (2 Corinthians 3:18).

To get to the next level of glory, we have to endure what the Bible calls, in 2 Corinthians 5:17, light afflictions: "For our light affliction, which is but for a moment, worketh for us a far more exceeding and eternal weight of glory." When the light affliction comes, always know that something is about to get better.

Force

The power of the Kingdom is force. Moses was a man who experienced the power of God throughout his life, from birth until death. Let me give you a little background on him. Moses was born to a Hebrew woman named Jochebed during the time the children of Israel were in slavery to the Egyptians. After many years of bondage, the Pharoah issued an order for all Hebrew baby boys to be thrown into the Nile because the Jews continued to multiply and multiply. Jochebed gave birth to Moses privately because, if the system had seen the boy, they would have destroyed him. At three months of age, Moses was set adrift in a basket in the Nile where an Egyptian princess pulled him out of the water and took him to her palace. His name, "Moses," means "drawn from the water." An interesting fact is that, at various times in Moses' life, he experienced miracles of water. One was the parting of the Red Sea so the Israelites could cross; he also struck a rock during the wilderness trek, and water came forth. Moses was gifted by God as a "water worker." His name was significant.

Moses was the man God chose to bring deliverance to His people, the children of Israel, who had been slaves to the Egyptians for 400 years. His ministry has been compared to that of Jesus in many ways. God called Moses to set captives free and to bring deliverance, a foreshadowing of Jesus, the Great Deliverer. Moses is known as the greatest prophet in the Old Testament; Jesus mentioned him more times than any other Old Testament figure because Moses brought order by ushering in the Mosaic law.

In Exodus 9:1, "The LORD said unto Moses, 'Go in unto Pharaoh, and tell him, Thus saith the LORD God of the Hebrews, Let my people go, that they may serve me.' " It would have been a good thing if the Pharaoh had just released the Israelites when Moses asked—but that didn't happen. God had to use a little "force" in the form of ten plagues described in Exodus 7–11 to persuade the Pharaoh that he meant what He said. Moses was a humble man. Numbers 12:3 says this about him—"Now the man Moses was very meek, above all the men which were upon the face of the earth."

In verses 6–8 of that same chapter, God continued,

> *"And he said, 'Hear my words: If there is a prophet*
> *among you, I the LORD will make myself known to him in a*
> *vision; I will speak with him in a dream. Not so with my*
> *servant Moses. He is faithful in all my house. With him I*
> *speak mouth to mouth, clearly, and not in riddles, and he*
> *beholds the form of the LORD.' "*

Moses was a meek, humble man, but that doesn't mean he was weak. It means he knew that the force needed to deliver God's people wouldn't come from him. He was the vessel that God chose to work through, and he was faithful to hear and obey His voice. The power of the kingdom is force and God is always on the lookout for a willing vessel.

When the devil took dominion over man at the time of Adam's fall, he imposed the culture of his satanic kingdom on humanity. This means satan "forced" his kingdom upon the earth. Let's look at an example in biblical culture using the book of Daniel to see how one culture can be imposed or forced upon another.

In Daniel 1, Nebuchadnezzar, king of Babylon, besieged Jerusalem. He then instructed his leaders to bring some of the children of Israel to serve in the king's palace in Babylon. Only the most skilled of the Jewish families, the king's seed, who were learned in science, math, architecture, and philosophy, were chosen. The Bible says that in Babylon they were renamed. Their language was taken away; their food and diet were changed. The Babylonian culture was forced upon the Jewish community. The imposition continued to also include worship. In Daniel 3:1, we read, "Nebuchadnezzar the king made an image of gold, whose height was threescore cubits, and the breadth thereof six cubits: he set it up in the plain of Dura, in the province of Babylon." In verses 4–5, the herald cried out, "…to you it is commanded, O peoples, nations, and languages, That at what time ye hear the sound of the cornet, flute, harp, sackbut, psaltery, dulcimer, and all kinds of musick, ye fall down and worship the golden image that Nebuchadnezzar the king hath set up: And whoso falleth not down and worshippeth shall the same hour be cast into the midst of a burning fiery furnace."

Only Daniel's three friends, Shadrach, Meshach, and Abednego, refused to bow down. That's because they made the decision according to Daniel 1:8 that they would not defile themselves by eating the delicacies at the king's table or accepting the king's dogma—"But Daniel purposed in his heart that he would not defile himself with the portion of the king's meat, nor with the wine which he drank…." Daniel and his friends refused to allow their culture to be replaced by the culture of the enemy.

When the British, French, and Portuguese came to Africa, and the Spanish and Portuguese went to South America, they took their cultures, their languages, their behavior, and their architecture and imposed it on the nations. Over the years, the original people group was diluted with the incoming groups, splitting the nation into different cultural groupings from a foreign land. They behaved so differently because a nation came and forced its culture upon a people.

Now listen: the satanic culture has been forced upon this world. In Genesis 1:28, after everything was created, this is what God did: "And God blessed them. And God said to them, "Be fruitful and multiply and fill the earth and subdue it, and have dominion over the fish of the sea and over the birds of the heavens and over every living thing that moves on the earth." He told us to subdue the earth and to take dominion. It is imperative that we realize that the command to be fruitful, multiply and take dominion has not changed. It was not diminished in spite of Adam's fall. That command was so important that God sent Jesus to redeem us from the curse of sin that Adam brought into the world, so that we once again would have the power to establish God's Kingdom as He instructed Adam to do. Jesus has given us the keys of the kingdom, and it's time to take it back. A generation IS coming that will impose the heavenly culture upon our earthly culture, replacing the demonic strongholds which have invaded and taken dominion over this world.

For increase to come to the Kingdom, we have to take action. Look at what Jesus told His followers in Matthew 11:12: "And from the days of John the Baptist until now the kingdom of heaven suffereth violence, and the violent take it by force." The word "force" can be translated "ardent zeal" or "intense exertion." Because satan has forced his culture on this world, it's our responsibility to aggressively and zealously take it back. Complacency has found its way into the church, allowing darkness to become greater and greater in today's society. In 2 Timothy we see this:

*This know also, that in the last days perilous times shall
come. For men shall be lovers of their own selves,
covetous, boasters, proud, blasphemers, disobedient to
parents, unthankful, unholy, Without natural affection,
trucebreakers, false accusers, incontinent, fierce,
despisers of those that are good, Traitors, heady, high
minded, lovers of pleasures more than lovers of God;
Having a form of godliness, but denying the power
thereof: from such turn away.*

The power of God cannot be denied if the Kingdom is to be increased. Proverbs 28:1 says, "...the righteous are bold as a lion." We must seize opportunities to reclaim and recover territory the enemy has taken. We must drive out darkness by ushering in Light, praying as Paul prayed in Ephesians 6:19–20, "... that words may be given to me in opening my mouth boldly to proclaim the mystery of the gospel, for which I am an ambassador in chains, that I may declare it boldly, as I ought to speak." Jesus said, "You will know the truth and the truth will set you free." Boldly, forcefully, zealously speak the truth in love and watch what happens. God will move in and take back territory the enemy has stolen.

Prayer is another way to take back the territory the enemy has stolen. Earlier I mentioned that ChiChi and I like to hold prayer meetings and seminars—do you know why? Prayer changes things! In Ezekiel 22:30, God said, "And I sought for a man among them that should make up the hedge, and stand in the gap before me for the land, that I should not destroy it: but I found none." He was looking for one man—just one pray-er who would save the land. James 5:16 tells us, "The effectual fervent prayer of a righteous man availeth much." There are over 500 verses on prayer in the King James Bible and about 650 prayers that were prayed. Prayer is a Biblical emphasis, one that has been overlooked for too long. The world's prayerlessness has produced a world in chaos—starving children, abused women, disease, pestilence, terrorism—heinous crimes against humanity abound as evil grows stronger with very little opposition. People don't pray. If they did, our world would look different. Prayer changes things. Stop right now and pray like you believe it.

Colossians 4:2 says, "Continue steadfastly in prayer, being watchful in it with thanksgiving." Keep praying; don't stop. Prayer is a force in the earth that will bring increase to His kingdom—it makes a difference.

In closing this section on force, let me admonish you to not only use force but also to be a "force"! Moses heard God and acted in faith to see captives set free. Daniel set his heart to choose God's culture over the satanic culture of the Babylonians. And Jesus prayed in Matthew 6:10, "Thy kingdom come, Thy will be done in earth, as it is in heaven." As we hear, obey, choose and pray, we can be part of the army that is mobilized in this generation to displace the darkness of this world with the Light of His kingdom. Do I hear an "Amen"?

Service
The culture of the Kingdom is service. Kingdom culture includes the beliefs, ideas, values, and knowledge which form a basis for action in the Kingdom. Service needs to be at the hub of everything we, as Believers, do because our actions should emulate those of Jesus our Savior who was the greatest Servant of all. Listen to this: Jesus emptied Himself to become like us in the form of a Servant according to Philippians 2:7—"Have this mind among yourselves, which is yours in Christ Jesus, who, though he was in the form of God, did not count equality with God a thing to be grasped, but emptied himself, by taking the form of a servant, being born in the likeness of men."

He is our Chief Cornerstone with His death and resurrection being the foundation of our faith, making service a primary building block of Kingdom living. Hear these words of Jesus in Matthew 20:26-28 as He addressed His disciples: "It shall not be so among you. But whoever would be great among you must be your servant, and whoever would be first among you must be your slave, even as the Son of Man came not to be served but to serve, and to give his life as a ransom for many" (ESV).

Look again at Philippians 2:7 and ask yourself, "What needs to be emptied out of me so I can conform to the image of a servant? Pride, I think, might be everyone's first choice. Self-serving might come next because He came to serve others, not Himself. Any number of things could come next—jealousy, hatred, judgementalism, etc. Make your list. If you're going to serve, your eyes can't keep looking at yourself, your circumstances, or your preferences….your eyes have to be on Him. If you were created in His image, there's a servant in there somewhere.

Below is a list of three levels of service we need to understand:
  1. **Serve your boss.** 1 Samuel 16:17–19, 21,22 relates how David served Saul:

> *And Saul said unto his servants, Provide me now a man that can play well, and bring him to me. Then answered one of the servants, and said, Behold, I have seen a son of Jesse the Bethlehemite, that is cunning in playing, and a mighty valiant man, and a man of war, and prudent in matters, and a comely person, and the Lord is with him. Wherefore Saul sent messengers unto Jesse, and said, Send me David thy son, which is with the sheep. And David came to Saul, and stood before him: and he loved him greatly; and he became his armour bearer. And Saul sent to Jesse, saying, Let David, I pray thee, stand before me; for he hath found favour in my sight.*

David came and served his boss, King Saul. He sang and the devil left. You serve your immediate superiors: your boss, your pastor, your bishop, your apostle. 1 Peter 2:18 says this: "Servants, be subject to your masters with all fear; not only to the good and gentle, but also to the froward."

David then went to another level of service when he fought Goliath in 1 Samuel 17:32: "And David said to Saul, Let no man's heart fail because of him; thy servant will go and fight with this Philistine." Of course the giant was killed, and David found favor in the sight of his "boss" and moved into the palace.

If you're going to advance in ministry, you must submit to someone. When Jesus came to John, John said, "You should be baptizing me…;" Jesus said, 'No, you're the senior priest; we have to fulfill righteousness; I'm submitted to you.' You have to serve someone. You are not authorized to go anywhere and start something if you haven't served someone, whether it's your boss, your people or your nation.

2. **Serve your nation.** These are the instructions Jesus gave His disciples in Matthew 10:5, "These twelve Jesus sent forth, and commanded them, saying, Go not into the way of the Gentiles, and into any city of the Samaritans enter ye not: But go rather to the lost sheep of the house of Israel." He is giving instruction to serve a nation. But later, in Mark 7:27–29, a Syrophenician woman came to him with a problem:

For a certain woman, whose young daughter had an unclean spirit, heard of him, and came and fell at his feet: The woman was a Greek, a Syrophenician by nation; and she besought him that he would cast forth the devil out of her daughter. But Jesus said unto her, Let the children first be filled: for it is not meet to take the children's bread, and to cast it unto the dogs. And she answered and said unto him, Yes, Lord: yet the dogs under the table eat of the children's crumbs. And he said unto her, For this saying go thy way; the devil is gone out of thy daughter.

The woman used wisdom to tie herself to the Jewish people through faith. She displayed the same faith Abraham used, allowing Jesus to work and serve His nation through her. We have to serve our nation or the nation God assigns us to.

3. **Serve your God.** Hebrews 12:28 says, "Wherefore we receive a kingdom which cannot be moved, let us have grace, whereby we may serve God acceptably with reverence and godly fear:" Paul said this in Romans 1:1 AMP: "Paul, a bondservant of Jesus Christ, called to be an apostle…" He said, "I'm a slave to God; The price over my head means that for the rest of my life, I'm a full slave." A big part of serving God is serving the body of Christ. If you love and serve Him, you've got to love and serve them!

"As we have therefore opportunity, let us do good unto all men, especially unto them who are of the household of faith" (Galatians 6:10). Serving God and serving man defines the culture of the Kingdom.

CHAPTER 7

STRUCTURE

The order of the Kingdom is structure. Structure is key to establishing generational purpose. Psalm 34:20 says, "He keeps all his bones; not one of them is broken." The bones in the human body actually mean structure. When the devil and his system plotted to destroy Jesus, His wounds were wounds of the flesh; they were not wounds that damaged the structure. Not a bone in His body was broken because the structure of the Kingdom of God was kept intact in His anointing. When we begin to build our lives, our families, our businesses, and our nation, there must be both order and structure.

There are three truths we need to learn about structure:
First, you have to build structure from the core:
    a) What are our core/fundamental beliefs? The reason the Body of Christ or the Church globally struggles is because we have so many evangelical/Pentecostal/charismatic/Orthodox/traditional church beliefs. We all believe different things about different things. Everybody believes differently about faith, the gifts, church order, baptism, etc.

I was in a certain place a few weeks ago and the teacher spent about 30 minutes preaching that you are baptized in your mother's womb. It was an interesting view, but Jesus was baptized of John. The Bible says that Jesus and His disciples baptized many. The Bible says that if you believe and you're baptized, you're saved. When you're in your mother's womb, you don't believe anything. You just believe that it's mealtime!

There are so many different views and beliefs about so many different things; and that creates numerous challenges. There are times we must set aside our petty differences and move forward. This is what Paul said about this in Hebrews 6:1–3:

> *So let us stop going over the basic teachings about Christ again and again. Let us go on instead and become mature in our understanding. Surely we don't need to start again with the fundamental importance of repenting from evil deeds and placing our faith in God. You don't need further instruction about baptisms, the laying on of hands, the resurrection of the dead, and eternal judgment. And so, God willing, we will move forward to further understanding."*

There are some beliefs, however, that are non-negotiable beliefs. Take, for instance, the doctrine of God, the virgin birth of Jesus, the sinless nature of Jesus, and His blood which is the atoning agent; all human beings are sinners and we must repent. These are non-negotiable doctrines. When we are building the structure, we must have solid <u>core</u> beliefs.

b) We need to know our core values. What are your core values? Core values include moral behavior, belief in the sanctity of life, certain freedoms in our nation, equality of men, etc. These are values formed from your belief in the Word as well as from your cultural upbringing. Core values lie at the center of your belief system.

c) We must establish core purposes. This has to do with your vision and your mission. There might be a mother out there who may never be the evangelist that goes around the world or the apostle that speaks on television or the prophet who prophesies to hundreds, but she understands her core purposes. She has three sons and has been instructed by the Holy Spirit to train those sons in the way they should go. This one will be the apostle that speaks to the nations; this is the one that evangelizes; and this is the one that's the prophet. Her core purpose is: "I'm going to cook for these kids; I'm going to clean their clothes; I'm going to help them with their homework. I will teach these young men, these young boys, to become men of value and valor. I'll be happy to have that as core purpose." Without Susanna Wesley's invaluable mothering, would John and Charles have become the note-worthy men they became?

d) We need to have a Biblical worldview—how we see the world, looking through the glasses of the Bible. The world's standards are constantly changing; the Bible's standards are not. The world employs situational ethics with evolving social mores. These shifting ideologies are re-shaping the world, and not in a good way! If we all viewed the world around us through a Biblical foundation, the result would be outstanding. A Biblical worldview is imperative. For example, on the agenda of the next council of African apostles, we're going to look at some of these non-negotiable Biblical principles to create a net of protection for the standards we hold. In the last 10–20–30 years, things that the church would not tolerate and stand for because of what we believe from the Bible are now being tolerated and are now being accepted. They are being framed into the culture of the church. Some of those things include homosexuality, same sex marriage and more.

When I was in the UK in August 2013, we learned about an agenda now being imposed on churches. In some places in the UK, pastors have been told they must recognize same sex marriage. For instance, if two men in a church feel they love each other and come to their pastor and say, "We've been members of this church for 7–8 years. We've discovered we love each other and we've been tithing faithfully and worshipping; we want to get married." The pastor must comply. If the pastor refuses to marry people that are members of his church, including men or women in same sex marriage, that pastor will then be prosecuted. Many, many churches are complying with this godless notion.

If you look on the tithing envelope in our church, we have written that all of your donations are freewill offerings, and you cannot claim them back. The reason that's necessary is because of an incident that happened a few years ago at a church in the United States. A woman was serving in a church and met some guy who became her boyfriend. She started having sex with this man before they were married, so the pastor chastised her for their sinful behavior. Based on the Word of God, sex outside of marriage is called fornication; in some cases, it's called adultery due to the nature of the sexual impropriety. The pastor was abiding by the statutes of the Bible and the church's bylaws. The offended woman sued the pastor and the church for infringing on her private life; the court ruled in her favor; and the church was forced to refund her all of her tithes and offerings for the year she was at the church, plus interest and damages. Ridiculous, and yet things of this nature are happening and in some places becoming the norm. The standard of righteousness is being challenged. Sin is being tolerated, even praised.

I was listening to an interview by a bishop of the Anglican Church and, in his interview, he made some shocking claims and declarations. He said he does not believe in God. He believes Jesus was a historical figure but Jesus was not God. He doesn't believe in the literal resurrection of Jesus but feels that the resurrection of Jesus is actually a metaphor that a human being can be raised from a lower standard of life into success. His beliefs were more universal beliefs as opposed to core beliefs. So basically, this Anglican bishop no longer believes in the accuracy and authority of the Word of God. Essentially he has created his own religion. It has evolved so far beyond basic Scriptural interpretation, it has become something else altogether.

If the structure of something is altered, its appearance changes. If the structure changes, the outcome changes. If the structure is not static, if it is pliable, if it is re-defined, then the result will be something different altogether.

The second way we build structure is that we have to structure apostolically. We are built on the foundation of apostles and prophets; there is an order to the team in which the ministry functions. There's got to be apostolic oversight; it's called *epi-sko-pas*, which means a central place for vision—the *epi-* center, the central place; and *sko-pas* means vision. 1 Corinthians 12:28 gives us the structure: "Now ye are the body of Christ, and members in particular. And God hath set some in the church, first apostles, secondarily prophets, thirdly teachers, after that miracles, then gifts of healings, helps, governments, diversities of tongues."

We have to be built structurally on apostolic oversight. The apostle is the lead. The person doesn't have to be named Apostle Bismark to be an apostle. I had a young man in New York come to me a while back who said, "Can you please release me as an apostle?" My answer was (and is) "No, I can't release you as an apostle! The Bible said, 'God gave some…' I can't make you an apostle." Ephesians 4:11 says, "And he gave some, apostles; and some, prophets; and some, evangelists; and some, pastors and teachers;" God gives; He decides; He releases.

Now there are things that I can give, positions I can appoint. I can appoint an elder, a deacon, a bishop. We ordain elders. We ordain deacons. We appoint and ordain bishops. I can give those positions, but I can't give the five-fold ministry. Now I can see into your life. I might see a "Timothy," assessing your calling according to the gifts God has given you. I can recognize, affirm, and nurture the gifts God has placed within you; I can give you my blessing and pray for you, but I can't make you a five-fold ministry gift.

God's design is that the structure of the church is built upon the apostle. Our church in Harare is built as an apostolic house led by an apostle with an apostolic team that oversees it. At some point, we have to hand this church over to someone else as the successor. That individual should have a strong apostolic mandate and gift on his life because if we hand it to someone else that doesn't have that, then the church is no longer led; the church is then managed. It's managed. There's a difference between a church being led and a church being managed. One of the primary issues the Western church faces today is its lack of apostolic oversight. We have pastors shepherding the sheep and managing the church organization but no apostle to connect and guide the heavenly mandate.

Moses led the children of Israel out of Egypt through the wilderness. When he handed his duties over to Joshua, Joshua settled the children of Israel in the land of Canaan. Joshua became the manager. He managed the land reform program in Israel. The land was taken from all the Hittites; Caleb was given a mountain somewhere in the Hebron district. After the management program of Joshua, there were no leaders in Israel. Not a single leader emerged because, without apostolic leadership, leaders will not emerge. When church leaders go into management mode, they won't produce apostolic leaders. And from Joshua to David, there were 300 years before a leader finally began to lead.

An apostolic team has a team of individuals that can help manage the ministry, but a manager cannot build apostolic leadership to lead the ministry. In the 21st century, the apostolic era has emerged and now has to assume leadership in every area of society. Apostolic leadership cannot be confined within the church; it must be present in every area of society and must be executed within the confines of Biblical structure.

How does that work? Well, it starts firstly with headship. Psalm 133:1–2 describes this: "Behold, how good and how pleasant it is for brethren to dwell together in unity! It is like the precious ointment upon the head, that ran down upon the beard, even Aaron's beard: that went down to the skirts of his garments…." Headship—it runs down the beard—that's leadership; then it runs onto the garments—that's fellowship. So headship is responsible for leadership. Once the oil goes on and establishes headship, it must go on to leadership, which is a product of the headship. Then it goes on the garment. The garment is fellowship. A mature church is where the fellowship has the same anointing as the headship. A mature church does as the bishop is doing. Now we have headship, leadership, and fellowship. When the oil is poured, it's not poured on the body; it's poured on the head. It's the head that is anointed.

When you have someone break away from a church, they cut themselves off from their head. How do you create another body? It is created through reproduction—not by amputation. If you want to start a church, it must be started through apostolic reproduction, not by cutting something off and sticking it in the ground by itself hoping it will grow.

We are all members of one body. How do we grow the body? We grow the body through covenant relationship. For instance, if Bishop makes you mad, you think, "I'm leaving this church; I'm going to start my own." You go find some tree somewhere and a bunch of tree-asmatics that are foolish enough to go with you and start a leaf ministry. Then you all become a bunch of fruits. Divisions and splits in the church have to stop. Don't leave a church just because you are unhappy. Don't dismember yourself just because everything isn't done the way you think it should be. Dismemberment is not the answer.

The church was created by God and He outlined a specific structure that must be followed if the body of Christ is to accurately represent the Kingdom of Heaven. Every body has a head, every head a spine, and every spine other bones that become the support system. Ministry must be developed in the same way. We must learn to demand structure and to honor its existence rather than buck against the system every time something rubs us the wrong way! If our churches are to be healthy, if they are to be effective and powerful, they must be structured Biblically, and as members we must support the structure!

The <u>third</u> area where you build structure is your family. Family has to be built with these four things in mind:

a) The core value is love. L-o-v-e. Husbands, love your wives. Ephesians 6:25 says, "Husbands, love your wives, even as Christ also loved the church, and gave himself for it…." Wives have to love their husbands. You have to love your children. Children have to love their parents. Do you know why? 1 Peter 4:8 tells us, "…love covers a multitude of sins." Love covers us and unites us as one entity, one body, and one family. When the husband as the head of the family loves them, a blessing of love is released to cover them all.

b) Honor is essential. The fifth commandment tells us to honor our father and mother—it's the first commandment with a blessing. Each family member, fathers, mothers, children, should outdo one another to show honor—"Love one another with brotherly affection. Outdo one another in showing honor." Romans 12:10

c) Always build generational thinking. The challenge we have as human beings is that everyone judges his life by "now." We just aren't programmed to think 10 years ahead. Ten years ago, some of you may have been in high school. When you were in high school, you wouldn't have dreamed that you'd be married and have children. Ten or so years from now, you'll be a grandfather. So the third thing you have to build in your family in terms of structure is a generational plan. How do you build that plan? You need a 10-year strategy with a strategy for each year. And every year of that 10-year strategy, you start adding another year. You need a plan for a tomorrow, then you need another plan, so that when you arrive at your tomorrow, you don't live on yesterday. You constantly have a tomorrow.

d) Establish core relationships. There was a pastor that I knew in Harare who had a very unfortunate thing happen in his church; it broke his heart. He died suddenly and left a wife with small kids. She was alone with no relationship, thinking that life was going to be forever with no relationships. When a crisis comes to your life, who are the people who can come immediately around you and be a support and a help?

You need core relationships, on three levels—those above you, those beside you, and those that you are mentoring, bringing up. Every family must have core relationships.

INCREASE OF THE KINGDOM

CHAPTER 8
GIFTS

The anointing of the kingdom is gifts. An organization, a church, or a ministry is only as powerful as its gifted people. We cannot develop and go further than the gift. There are times when God will bring an anointing that can override a person's limitations or a person's incompetence, but that's not the way God functions in a long-term manner. There are times, for example, when God will anoint a person and they'll preach an outstanding message without having done too much research or study. That becomes the exception to the rule. The rule, according to 2 Timothy 2:15, is to, "Study to shew thyself approved unto God, a workman that needeth not to be ashamed, rightly dividing the word of truth." You have to make preparation. There are times when the anointing can fall on a person, and they'll be able to minister in song, or maybe, within a prophetic range outside of their natural gifting, but that's the exception to the rule. God will usually work within the gifting of the individual.

In Solomon's day, God gave Solomon a mandate to build the temple which would be the place where God would dwell. Although the money was there for the temple, Solomon found people outside of Israel who had skills to come in to help build it according to 1 Kings 7:13, 14: "And King Solomon sent and fetched Hiram out of Tyre. He was a widow's son of the tribe of Naphtali, and his father was a man of Tyre, a worker in brass: and he was filled with wisdom, and understanding, and cunning to work all works in brass. And he came to King Solomon, and wrought all his work."

If we don't have the skill or competencies or the gift within our immediate range, we then have to go outside of our immediate family and employ that skill to improve the product. There are a number of things here about the kingdom of God and giftedness that are important.

The first thing that I want to mention is that your gift will discover you. Many times that shows forth before you show up. When David's gift came to the forefront in 1 Samuel 16:17, David's gift discovered him. Saul asked for a musician. "Then answered one of the servants, and said, Behold, I have seen a son of Jesse the Bethlehemite, that is cunning in playing...."

According to Proverbs 18:16, "A man's gift maketh room for him, and bringeth him before great men." So, **secondly**, that gift that God has given you, as it leads you to great people, will make room for you. Many times, however, our gift comes like a diamond in the rough. It just needs to be trimmed or cut or shaped. Your gift is like clay; it's on the wheel but the vessel has to be shaped. Your gift is a raw material that has to be processed into a finished product. It's the road to discovery because the more your gift is under pressure, the more of the real you begins to come into full profile and manifestation.

As your gift makes room for you, you have to make room for your gift. As your gift makes room for you, it can only make room for you according to the way you've made room for it. You can have someone that's an intellectual, that's an academic, but without putting your gift through different levels of schooling, you can never be very successful. You can have a person who's highly academic and should be a Ph.D., but only made room for their gift to a Grade 7 education. It's not your gift's fault; it's your fault that you haven't made room for your gift. If you make room for your gift, your gift then makes room for you. They work together.

Thirdly, your gift will create, what I call, the sphere of a person. You might have somebody who is gifted, but it takes time for the sphere of their gifting to be activated and released. A sphere is a place, a measure of a region of a person's influence or impact. The more impactful you become with your gift, the more your influence increases. When David took on Goliath and slayed the giant, his gift made room for him. David's sphere was that of a giant killer. But, as the years went by, David's sphere increased with every battle that he fought and every victory that he won. He was then gaining others' influence in his sphere of influence.

Let's look at another scriptural basis to support the idea of increasing your sphere of influence. This is taken from 1 Chronicles 4:10 NKJV: "And Jabez called on the God of Israel saying, "Oh, that You would bless me indeed, and enlarge my territory, that Your hand would be with me, and that You would keep me from evil, that I may not cause pain!" So God granted him what he requested." The name "Jabez" meant his mother bore him in pain. Jabez wanted to change his impact on society. He cried out to God for help in that area, and God did it. We aren't told exactly how that happened, but God granted his request. So if you want to change your area of influence and enlarge your territory, tell God— He will direct your steps to make that come to pass.

Levels of Impact

The definition of the word "impact" is an "action of one object coming forcibly into contact with another." The second definition of impact is "marked effect or influence." It's a marked effect or influence, an impression that produces a dramatic, notable or sizeable result.

Listed below are eight levels of impact:

1. **No impact.** We will do a case study on the life of Jacob. There are actually a lot of people in the world, even in church or in ministry, who are no-impact people. In Genesis 30:22–24, we read that Rachel after being barren for many years gave birth to Joseph: "Then God remembered Rachel, and God listened to her and opened her womb. And she conceived and bore a son, and said, "God has taken away my reproach." So she called his name Joseph, and said, "The LORD shall add to me another son.""

It says she called his name Joseph. Notice that Jacob didn't say that; Rachel said that. Jacob didn't name any of the first four of his sons. His first son was Reuben; his second was Simeon; third was Levi; and fourth was Judah, all named by Leah, his wife. It was the father's job to name kids, but his wives named those boys. In my opinion, that shows Jacob had no impact because he didn't assume the headship position. He didn't assume his responsibility. We read in Genesis 29 that, because Rachel didn't have children and Leah did, she took her servant, Bilhah, and gave her to Jacob. Jacob had two sons with the first servant. Then Leah gave her servant, Zilpah, and she had two sons. So Jacob doesn't name any of the kids. The only child that Jacob named was Benjamin. When Benjamin was named, Rachel was dying. Genesis 35:17–19a tells it like this: "Now it came to pass, when she was in hard labor, that the midwife said to her, "Do not fear; you will have this son also." And so it was, as her soul was departing (for she died), that she called his name Ben-Oni; but his father called him Benjamin. So Rachel died and was buried…"

There were points in Jacob's life when he was a man of no impact. You cannot live your life with no impact. The day Joseph was born was the day that changed his life. See the account in Genesis 30:25–28:

And it came to pass, when Rachel had borne Joseph, that Jacob said to Laban, "Send me away, that I may go to my own place and to my country. Give me my wives and my children for whom I have served you, and let me go; for you know my service which I have done for you. And Laban said to him, "Please stay, if I have found favor in your eyes, for I have learned by experience that the LORD has blessed me for your sake." Then he said, "Name me your wages, and I will give it."

Laban understood the blessing that Jacob brought to his house and was unwilling to give it up. He even offered to increase Jacob's wages if he would stay. While Jacob was in the realm of no-impact for about 20 years, the system was telling him what it wanted him to do. But the day he shifted to become a man of impact is the day his life changed.

2. **The second level of impact is an event that changes your vision.** It's impact that changes your vision. When Joseph was born, Jacob saw himself in that baby. That was the impact or the event that changed his vision. If you are a person that has no impact, you have to pray that God will give you an event that will change your vision. You can be at a certain place at a certain time and something happens to your life. Your life becomes impacted, and your vision changes. Or perhaps a person comes into your life at a certain time who speaks a word of counsel or advice or a prophetic word that will change your vision and move you from a no-impact person to an impact person.

Many years ago, an event changed my vision. Up until that point, I was a person who had minimal impact and an ineffective ministry. In 1978, I was in the city of Durban, South Africa, and there was a pastor there named Nelson Haynes. I preached in his church conference, then in his church. One night after midnight, he took me to a place that's still there in Durban called the Blue Lagoon. It's the place where the Umgeni flows into the Indian Ocean. There was a full moon; the sky was vivid blue, and the ocean waves were cresting on the rocks in the Blue Lagoon. As those waves were cresting, Pastor Haynes spoke a word into my life about my future and my destiny. It was a completely unexpected moment, one that I will never forget. That event, that prophetic word of counsel and relationship, literally changed my vision.

There must be impact that changes your vision. Unless your vision changes, you'll perish. Proverbs 29:18 tells us, "Where there is no vision, the people perish: but he that keepeth the law, happy is he." Vision is the first thing that has to happen in your life. Habakkuk 2:3, 4 says, "And the LORD answered me, and said, Write the vision, and make it plain upon tables, that he may run that readeth it." You have to write that vision and make it plain. So if you are a no-impact person, pray that God will send you an event or an individual to change your level of impact.

Experience can also change your vision. You may have a time when an occasion arises within you that says, "This is how I want to be!" The experience might come through something you see on television, or through a magazine you're reading. You might read a biography or see a movie about someone who has made an impact on society in sports, television, the arts, etc. When you witness something that challenges your paradigm or presses your limits, the exposure to that experience and the possibilities that exist changes your vision. The experience activates something that resides within your heart and in your spirit.

3. **The third level of impact is impact that changes your behavior.** It's one thing to have your vision changed, but you now have to have your behavior changed. When Jacob's vision changed, he was impacted to the point where he said, "I've got to leave," and his behavior began to change. In Genesis 30: 29–30, "Jacob said to him, "You yourself know how I have served you, and how your livestock has fared with me. For you had little before I came, and it has increased abundantly, and the LORD has blessed you wherever I turned. But now when shall I provide for my own household also?" Laban continues to ask him in verse 31, "What shall I give you?" Laban was begging him to stay. Jacob had a plan and this is what he said in Genesis 30:31–34:

> *You shall not give me anything. If you will do this for*
> *me, I will again pasture your flock and keep it: let*
> *me pass through all your flock today, removing from*

*it every speckled and spotted sheep and every black
lamb, and the spotted and speckled among the goats,
and they shall be my wages. So my honesty will
answer for me later, when you come to look into my
wages with you. Every one that is not speckled and
spotted among the goats and black among the lambs,
if found with me, shall be counted stolen." Laban
said, "Good! Let it be as you have said."*

So Laban is astounded that this man doesn't want anything; and
Laban thinks this is a brilliant deal. Jacob doesn't want wages;
he doesn't want anything; all he wants is to separate the cattle
three days apart and those that have plain coats will be with him,
and if they give birth to cattle with patches or different coats,
those will be Jacob's. Laban thinks, "This boy's more stupid than
I thought," because genetically, biologically, that cannot happen.
But the thing is, Jacob was impacted on the third level of impact.
His vision changed; and now his behavior's going to change.

He is no longer working as a laborer; he's now functioning as
an entrepreneur. His behavior is no longer that of a worker with
appointed wages. His behavior now is, "I'm an entrepreneur. I'm
working for myself, my wives, and my children." So behavior
has to change—impact that changes behavior.

You might wake up in the morning and say, "I now understand
that for that position I want, whether it's in the financial sector
or the political sector, or the education sector, I need to go to a
higher school of learning. Having that vision is one thing, but
behavior is another.

In my own circumstances I was in my mid-40's, when I knew
and I purposed in my heart that I wanted to get my own earned
degree before I turned 50. That was my vision. My vision had
changed. Next, I had to have impact that changed my behavior,

so I applied to a school to get a degree in business administration. I began reading and studying books. I understood there were some things that had to go—T.V., movies, all of that had to go. For almost 3 ½ years, every day including Sundays, I'd get up at two o'clock in the morning, no matter where I was in the world. Sometimes I would work all night. Behavior has to change so you can get a result. It's not enough just to have a vision, behavior has to change.

I've been around some pretty profound people. I know when Kirk Franklin was doing his album, "Revolution," and when Israel Houghton was getting ready for his album, "South Africa—Live in South Africa," both guys, months and months before their recordings were spending hours, sometimes 20 hours a day in the studio, practicing and working on those pieces.

If you're going to be successful in life and if your gift is going to make room for you, your vision must be impacted. Next, your behavior must be impacted. Behavior has to change. You cannot have a different result with the same behavior.

4. **The fourth level of impact is impact that changes or alters your destiny.** Even if your behavior changes, it may not alter your destiny. There's got to be impact that alters your destiny. You have to have a destination to have a destiny.

ChiChi and I were in Zambia in September, 2012 because I'd been asked to perform a wedding for Dr. Nevers Mumba's son. The bride was late, which is not unusual, but she was extraordinarily late, which, for one of the very few times in my life, we really appreciated. The reason was that President Kaunda was at the wedding, and we were sitting in the private lounge with him.

The bride was three hours late so we had 2-1/2 hours with President Kaunda. We took pictures with him and had a chance to talk with him. I said to him, "Mr. President, do you mind if I ask you a couple of questions." He said, "Oh, no, no, no…." Of course I told him that ChiChi was Zambian so he said, "Did you come and get your land?" You know that generation, they love their land!

So I asked him a couple of questions during our conversation. I have my personal commitment to see Africans empowered, not just to have a house or a car but to own the continent, so I asked him a question. I said, "Mr. President, where did you get that statement, 'One Zambia, One Nation,'" because that statement 'One Zambia, One Nation' is very patristic. It is also a statement that, in my opinion, was ahead of its time because when it was released in 1963–64, many people didn't grasp the weight of that statement. The President shared this story with me which I'll now share with you after obtaining his permission.

He said that his parents were strong missionaries, Christian believers. He said it came to him that he would possibly be the first President of an independent Zambia from the colonial era. The impact of that thought altered his vision. Next, he had to get some training, formal training. That's behavior, so you have impact that altered his behavior. He said because there was destiny, they prayed and asked God what they should do for the nation of Zambia.

He said, at that time, there were 75 different tribal groupings and many, many different linguistic groupings in Zambia, so there could be challenges. Those were in addition to the various white groupings from Europe, Asia, India and Pakistan. Just counting indigenous Zambian people, there were 75 different groupings. Because it was such a diverse nation, the Lord led them to a Scripture that said, "You shall love the Lord your God with all your heart, your mind, your soul, your strength," and the second part, "and your neighbor as yourself." That verse is from Matthew 22:37. He said they took, "Love your neighbor as yourself," and said, "If we are going to be a successful Zambia, we have to be One Zambia, One Nation." Now, that's powerful.

It was a statement that impacted destiny. You have to have impact that will impact destiny. So then, not only do you have to move from a no-impact person to impact that impacts your vision and impact that changes behavior—you have to move to impact that alters destiny.

The Bible says that when the cattle were harvested in Jacob's life after one year, Jacob was very blessed. In Genesis 30:43, the Bible says, "And the man increased; he grew in wealth; he became very rich in cattle; he became very rich in herds, in flocks, in menservants, maidservants, camels and donkeys." Look at the Word, "He increased exceedingly...." In fact, this guy made more in the 21st year he was there than he made in the first 20 years put together! When Jacob landed at Laban's place, and he saw Rachel, the man was so in love, he worked for seven years with no money for a woman. And when he woke up the next morning with a hangover from the celebration the night before, he recognized that this wasn't Rachel. It was her sister, Leah. So he worked another seven years for Rachel. That adds up to 14 years with no pay. He worked 14 years for one woman. And then he worked another six years after Joseph was born. Jacob was in Laban's house for 20 years. In the 21st year, which is the 3rd seven of his life at Laban's place, the third cluster of sevens, he increased exceedingly. In Genesis 31:5–7 it says,

So Jacob sent and called Rachel and Leah into the field where his flock was and said to them, "I see that your father does not regard me with favor as he did before. But the God of my father has been with me. You know that I have served your father with all my strength, yet your father has cheated me and

changed my wages ten times. But God did not permit
him to harm me.

The brothers of Rachel and Leah came to them and said, "Your husband has taken all of what was our father's." They recognized that, if Jacob left, everything they'd enjoyed for 21 years would leave with him.

Jacob made a decision that made an impact that was going to change his destiny. Now watch why this is important. If he stayed where he was, he would not become what he should become. That leads me to impact No. 5.

5. **The fifth level of impact is impact that makes waves.** When he made the decision, "I'm leaving," it made waves everywhere. There are times when you have to make sound decisions concerning what you have to do; and sometimes, family members are not happy. You will make waves. You will go separate ways with siblings, brothers or sisters, people you've been with for many, many years. It just makes waves. When you decide, in my case as a church leader, that your church is going to take on a certain frame, people will leave you; it makes waves. In 1988, I'd just come back from a series of conferences in the U.S. When we got back from those conferences, I began to teach in our church something that created a lot of problems; it made waves.

Africa is comprised of many different people groups; they're called races or racial groupings. I am in the colored racial grouping or colored people. In South Africa, it's more accentuated. In Zambia, Malawi and everywhere you have British rule, you have racial groupings. You have whites; you have coloreds; you have Asians; and then you have indigenous African people. When you fill out a form for government or business, etc., there is always a place you have to put your race. When I filled out the form, I'd put "human race;" I got into trouble because they thought I was being sarcastic.

I learned that you're either black or you're white. It's true that there is a racial grouping of colored people; and they do have their own behavior and way they do things. But I taught our colored church (it was 98% colored back then) that we were black people, and I had many, many people from the colored community in our church leave. Many left because they wanted to be colored and not black. It caused us a lot of problems and many challenges. It affected our finances at that immediate time; it affected/changed the way we taught and the way we understood. It changed a lot of things in our lives. That's just one example of how an impact can make waves.

6. **The sixth level of impact is impact that creates impacters.** When Jacob left Laban's place, please remember this: the man had 11 sons; and his oldest sons were probably in their late teens. The Bible says in Genesis 37:3, that Joseph was the son of Jacob's old age. "Now Israel loved Joseph more than any other of his sons, because he was the son of his old age." Joseph was born when Jacob was an old man.

In Genesis 31:3, "The LORD said to Jacob, 'Return to the land of your fathers and to your kindred, and I will be with you.' " Jacob was going to see his father in Genesis 31:17,18—"So Jacob arose and set his sons and his wives on camels. He drove away all his livestock, all his property that he had gained, the livestock in his possession that he had acquired in Paddan-aram, to go to the land of Canaan to his father Isaac."

All of Jacob's kids aligned themselves to their dad's decision because they recognized the blessing on his life. Jacob impacted impacters. He put into these men the power to become heads of tribes. The Bible says in Acts 7:9, "And the patriarchs, jealous of Joseph, sold him into Egypt; but God was with him." The "patriarchs" in that passage refers to Joseph's brothers. They became known as patriarchs because one man impacted impacters. It's not enough just to have impact in your life, your vision, or your destiny. You can become the role model that impacts many. You become the prototype whose footsteps many will follow. Impacters impact individuals and cause those people to flow in a distinct level of force. Who are you impacting? Who are you influencing that they become impacters?

7. **The seventh level of impact is impact that influences generations**. It's not enough just to impact impacters; we have to influence generations. Daniel 4:3—"...dominion is from generation to generation." So if you look at the life of Jacob here, not only did he create impacters but also his impact was going to influence generations.

8. **The eighth level of impact is impact that changes the world— it makes history**. I do understand that this is a level that can be very thin where there are only a handful of people who can rise to this level. I understand that. But it doesn't mean that everybody in the room can't desire to attain the level of a history maker or a global phenomenon where, in some way, you can change the trajectory of the human family as a whole. Perhaps you at least desire to impact your family, your tribe, or your nation. You can have that desire. I've been in the presence of many individuals who have phenomenal anointing; but also I've been in the room with individuals whose lives changed the world. There is a difference.

I met an amazing, very popular pastor at one time and thought, "Wow, this is incredible." What an incredible man with a wonderful, incredible global anointing. But then I met his spiritual father and mentor, who was Kenneth Copeland. There was a difference: The first guy had a great anointing—so does Kenneth Copeland, but Copeland has changed the world. There's a difference. When you come into the presence of someone who changed the world, it's amazing.

In my short lifetime, I've had the privilege of meeting all kinds of people. I met President Mandela in 1998, and just those 30 seconds—30 seconds—changed my life. I met Yasser Arafat; it totally changed my life. I didn't agree with some of his viewpoints, but that's a different story. It just changed my life. Sisters and brothers, there's a difference between somebody that impacts impacters and someone who influences generations and changes the world. There's a real difference.

When you've decided in your heart that you will be a world changer, you have to push until you get there. Everybody reading or hearing this message knows what level of impact you need to implement right now. You know what level you have to do, and if you are at the level where you are a no-impact person, you have to mobilize your gift to the point where you have impact that changes your vision.

Once you have impact that changes your vision, you cannot remain there. You have to have impact that changes your behavior. If you keep on giving a bad product to your clientele, they'll stop buying your product, whether it's bread, milk, or a service you provide. Every time you give bad service, you are diminishing your ability to have impact.

On the other hand, every time you render a good service, you are increasing your ability to be a high impact person. Let's deal with King David and King Saul. Saul had the potential to be high impact, but unfortunately, Saul was no-impact. Saul did not positively impact anybody, not a single person. He destroyed his natural sons; he destroyed his spiritual sons; he destroyed priests; he destroyed a nation. Saul was a no-impact person. When David came into Saul's life, he entered as a no-impact person and left as a man that made history—a world changer.

The Apostle Paul, who is the apostle to the Gentiles, was a no-impact person when he began. On the road to Damascus, his life changed—he encountered impact that changed his vision. He got to the city of Damascus where Ananias prayed for him. Scales fell off Paul's eyes and the impact that changed his vision began changing his behavior. He started preaching, and that is changed behavior. He then had to leave the city and go to the desert for three and a half years to study. That became impact that changed destiny.

When he left the desert and headed to Tarsus, he started his ministry. He then became an impacter that created impacters. Acts 16 tells how he met and recruited young Timothy. He said in various passages that there was no one like Timothy. He had Titus, his spiritual son, as well as Euodious, Trophimus, Tychicus, and Secundus. All of these individuals became men he impacted.

Then he impacted generations. Timothy became the bishop of the churches in Asia Minor with headquarters in Ephesus. Titus became the bishop of all the Mediterranean islands. He made impacters that still are impacting generations. Even today, the life of the Apostle Paul is still influencing the nations. He was a global impacter that changed the world.

The anointing of the Kingdom of God hangs on your gift. Everyone has been gifted in some way. What you do with it is up to you. How you develop it is up to you. How far you want to go is up to you. We find a real skill and gift deficiency especially in the body of Christ. That's why we have low impact because we have people who won't improve their gifts. They're waiting for somebody to nudge them. The anointing of the Kingdom is giftedness and gifted people.

CHAPTER 9
GENERATIONAL DOMINION, FAITH & UNITY

The success of the Kingdom is generational dominion. True success is found in identifying and training up successors. I've read that there are different catalogs of what is called apostolic succession that date back over a 1,000 years with one dating back over 1,700 years. In the Catholic Church, there are distinct lines of succession, with one apostle passing on to the next and so on. That's why they're still here. A challenge for the 21st century, especially for the Pentecostal/Charismatic church, is the lack of succession planning.

Africa, as a continent, does not think succession. We see this not only in Zimbabwe but also in Africa as a whole. We see this in our politics. I think the only country that has had a really disciplined democratic succession program is Botswana, where there's been changing of the guard or passing power to the next president without incident. I can't think of any African country, except Botswana, that has had success with succession in the political world.

You also don't see that type of planning in Africa in the business world, outside of white people who have had five to six centuries' head start on indigenous black people. You do see succession in Africa amongst chieftainships. For example, Chief So-and-So is succeeded by his son who becomes the next chief. That's true on a tribal level, but it's confined within a tribal setting. That has been successful there; but on a broader scale, a national scale, you don't see too much of it.

How then, do we plan for generational dominion?
The following five points give you steps to guide you through
developing succession:

1. **You must develop the idea of succession.** The success of the
   Kingdom of God as a whole is based on generational dominion.
   When one generation gains dominion, it must not hold on to
   power without passing it on to the next. The idea of succession
   has to be built into the framework of our ministries before we
   can implement succession. We have to have a forward thinking
   mindset with a vision for the future.

   Somehow we feel that we're going to live forever. Everybody
   judges their life by "now". We live by "now," and we forget 10,
   20, 30, or 40 years from now. When I first started preaching in
   1974, I would never, ever have thought that the year 2014 would
   come. In 1974, to even think of the year 2000 was impossible.
   It was impossible to think 2000. In fact, in 1974, it was hard to
   even think as far as 1980.

   When Zimbabwe became independent in 1980, on the 18th of
   April, the President made his inaugural speech. I was watching
   him on television and listening to the repeats on radio for days
   and weeks following. They were talking about ten years in the
   future, 1990, when the 20% of the Zimbabwean government was
   mandatory, compulsory whites. The Rhodesian Front had to have
   20%, so there was no overall majority in Parliament of black
   people to overrule the Lancaster Agreement. They were talking
   about 1990, when that piece would fall away, and Zimbabwe
   then would be truly democratic. It was 1980—you couldn't even
   think 1990, let alone the year 2000.

   People think "now." You don't even have children yet, but 20
   years from now, you may have an 18-year-old son and a 17-year-
   old daughter and a 16-year-old son. But you're thinking "now."

When you think in the "now," you eliminate the possibility of succession. So we have to develop the idea of succession in our culture—at least the idea of it.

I was in the United State in October 2013 and had two significant experiences. The first one was at Bishop Ralph Dennis' church, where he was handing his ministry over to his son. His third son, Bishop Gregory Dennis, was being handed the baton for that church. Bishop Ralph Dennis was 65 years old. His son was somewhere in his early 40's. It was an exhilarating experience, witnessing a father, at a time in his life when he was still strong, still with energy, hand over his ministry to a living son.

In the same course of travels, I came to another place where a man, now 78, was asking me if I could please help them find a pastor for his church because he had no successor. The opportunity to hand his ministry over to his son passed 15 or 20 years ago. When the opportunity came, he did not do that when he could have. Now when he's fading into the sunset as a wonderful warrior that's given so much to the body of Christ, his success has grossly diminished because he has no successor. He asked me in Zimbabwe, Africa to help him find a successor, when, in fact, his ministry started 60 years ago, before I was even born.

We must develop the idea of succession.

2. **You must construct the framework of succession.** The Bible's clear. Paul said this in Titus 2:3–5:

> *The aged women likewise, that they be in behaviour*
> *as becometh holiness, not false accusers, not given*
> *to much wine, teachers of good things; That they*
> *may teach the young women to be sober, to love*
> *their husbands, to love their children, to be discreet,*

chaste, keepers at home, good, obedient to their own
husbands, that the word of God be not blasphemed.

"Let the older women teach the younger." It's not just talking, teaching them how to have a baby, how to look after their husband, how to sew a button on a shirt, or how to do homework with the kids—that's not the whole idea of mentoring. The whole idea here is creating succession so that what our godly women know today will be imparted to the next generation who will do even better in the future. We build on one another's shoulders, putting together the nuts and bolts of a framework. That is imperative in preparing for succession.

3. **You must develop how you walk it out.** How do we walk out succession? We plan and think through the range of possible scenarios, identifying potential challenges. For example, if I hand this ministry over, and there is a failure, how do we fix the failure? If there's infiltration...what happens next? We have to look at all kinds of options. We must walk it out in a planning phase before we actually do it.

4. **You must identify successors.** Chapter 16 is a wonderful chapter of the Book of Acts. Paul was preaching at a certain place and saw a young man there, probably about sixteen years old. This is the account from Acts 16:1–3:

Then came he to Derbe and Lystra: and, behold, a
certain disciple was there, named Timotheus, the
son of a certain woman, which was a Jewess, and
believed; but his father was a Greek: Which was well
reported of by the brethren that were at Lystra and
Iconium. Him would Paul have to go forth with him;
and took and circumcised him because of the Jews
which were in those quarters: for they knew all that
his father was a Greek.

Paul said, "I've gotta have that boy. I've gotta have him." In 1 Timothy 1:2, he called him his son. He also called Titus his son in Titus 1:4. Although some forsook Paul, many such as Epaphras, Epaphroditus, Priscilla and Acquilla—they stood with him. These were successors that Paul had identified.

In Acts 20:3, Paul went to Asia. The Spirit had previously constrained him and forbidden him to go into Asia, but now in Acts 20:3, Paul made his decision to go. Take note of who he's going into Asia with because he had identified successors: "And there accompanied him into Asia Sopater of Berea; and of the Thessalonians, Aristarchus and Secundus; and Gaius of Derbe, and Timotheus; and of Asia, Tychicus and Trophimus." These were individuals that Paul had identified as successors.

When Jesus launched his ministry, He identified His successors. Matthew 4:18–22:

And Jesus, walking by the sea of Galilee, saw two brethren, Simon called Peter, and Andrew his brother, casting a net into the sea: for they were fishers. And he saith unto them, Follow me, and I will make you fishers of men. And they straightway left their nets, and followed him. And going on from thence, he saw other two brethren, James the son of Zebedee, and John his brother, in a ship with Zebedee their father, mending their nets; and he called them. And they immediately left the ship and their father, and followed him.

He said, "Follow me." So Jesus identified His successors as He began His ministry.

5. You must perform the act of succession. Years ago in Mombasa, we had a very powerful father-son summit where I met some iconic Africans who had built formidable ministries. Some were in their late 70's, and many of their sons were there. Several leaders gave presentations, with mine being one of the final ones; I was talking about different aspects of succession. When we had our lunch break, somebody around the table shared his idea of succession. He believed that, in the first generation, a man must stay there for a very long time until he's 80 or 90 years of age, then hand it over. He felt a ministry could really only take root after 40 years of being established. Of course, I didn't agree, and I told him I didn't agree—just in discussion. As the years have gone by, I've since spoken to the same individual who has dramatically had a change of mind on succession.

You get to a certain age in your life where you can't do what you used to do in the way you used to do it. Suddenly, you realize you're going to need some help. So the first four steps I gave you are important; but what has to happen while you're still strong is that you have to perform the act of succession. You have to hand over so that you run together with your successor for a while.

The success of the Kingdom is generational dominion and it's built on the backdrop of succession. We must make sure that what we establish here on this level in this era is handed to the next generation so they can go further faster.

Faith

The currency of the Kingdom is faith. We will begin with a quick overview of faith. Faith is belief, of course, but the Bible uses the word "faith" in the New Testament in several interchangeable ways. There are three things regarding faith that we'd like to explore:

1. We find in Hebrews 11:6 that "Without faith it is impossible to please God...." The word "faith" in this verse refers to our trust in Him, our belief that He is God. Take a look at four references in the New Testament utilizing that kind of faith:

a) "So then faith cometh by hearing, and hearing by the word of God." Romans 10:17. Hearing the Word increases faith that pleases God.

b) Romans 10:8—"But what saith it? The word is nigh thee, even in thy mouth, and in thy heart: that is, the word of faith, which we preach." This is the Word in our heart and mouth, which is also what we preach.

c) "Let us hold fast the profession of our faith without wavering; (for he is faithful that promised;)…" Hebrews 10:23 tells us to hold fast to our faith.

d) "For verily I say unto you, That whosoever shall say unto this mountain, Be thou removed, and be thou cast into the sea; and shall not doubt in his heart, but shall believe that those things which he saith shall come to pass; he shall have whatsoever he saith." Jesus made this statement to His disciples in Mark 11:23, teaching us to confess our faith to move mountains. That's faith to believe for things to happen.

2. There's a second way the word "faith" is used. The apostle in Jude 1:3b wrote: "I found it necessary to write appealing to you to contend for the faith that was once for all delivered to the saints." Faith is used here to represent a fundamental, theological belief or principle. It's doctrinal faith.

So what do we believe? We believe fundamentally: There is a God. We believe in Jesus, born of a virgin, who ministered in the earth, and was crucified and buried; the third day He rose again and sits on the right hand of the Father. That's what we believe. It's this core faith in our beliefs that makes us Christians. It's a fundamental faith that we do not forsake. The Bible says, when Paul was writing to Timothy in 1 Timothy 4:1, "Now the Spirit speaketh expressly, that in the latter times some shall depart from the faith, giving heed to seducing spirits, and doctrines of devils;" The "faith" in that passage means "core beliefs." There are seducing spirits that take people away from the core, fundamental belief of doctrine and theology. Paul tells his spiritual son in 2 Timothy 4:2, "Preach the word; be instant in season, out of season; reprove, rebuke, exhort with all long suffering and doctrine."

Paul said, "Preach the word" because the Word of God is good for reproof and correction. These are things that are fundamental beliefs.

3. There's a third word for faith found in 1 Corinthians 12, starting from verse 8. It's called the gift of faith. The gift of faith is just that—a gift! God gives it sovereignly to an individual because He is good, not because of anything we have done. This is not faith that comes by hearing and hearing by the word of God. This is not faith that comes through fundamental, core beliefs. This is a gift.

I've seen people with a gift of faith. Miracles happen as a result of the gift of faith. In my own life, the gift of faith has come upon me at various times in various places. It's not something that sits on me 24/7 every day as it does on some people in the world. But every now and then, the gift of faith will come upon me and I've seen tremendous, miraculous things take place.

I remember the first time I experienced the gift of faith in 1975. We had a church bus; and my mom used to drive it with me sitting right next to her as she drove. I used to change the gears for her because the steering was so heavy; she'd put the clutch in, and I'd change the gears.

We used to have street services in a place called Thorn Grove in the city of Bulawayo, Zimbabwe. One night we had a street service outside the home of an elderly lady named Sis Francis.

And what a powerful street service it was; it was powerful! I'll never forget it.

Sis Francis had a son who lived adjacent to her, and he was very sick. He was an alcoholic whose body had been poisoned through alcohol. We went to pray for him because they said he was dying. His pain was excruciating, and to demonstrate just how bad it was, his wife took a piece of tissue and touched his stomach. When the tissue hit his stomach, he started screaming because it felt like a bucket of bricks that hit him in his stomach. He wasn't well. They sang songs and began to pray for him. After they had prayed, I suddenly began to speak. My mother grabbed my hand because I was probably the second youngest there, around 17 or 18 years of age; and kids are not supposed to speak when there are adults in serious ministry.

The Spirit of God spoke to me, and I said to him, "Uncle Paul, the Lord is healing you now. You are healed now, and if you go back to your lifestyle, a worse sickness will come on you." The next morning when we drove to pick up the people at the bus stop at Sis Francis' home, we ran in to see him. He was totally healed. The previous night after we left, he started going to the toilet, and out of him was coming a black tar. The poison was coming out of him, and he was totally healed.

My mom asked him, "Are you coming to church?" and he said, "Ay, no, no, no…no, no, no." He kept on with the same lifestyle in spite of God's warning. Fast forward to about 10 years later—ChiChi and I were married and I was in Bulawayo with my dad. We were walking down the street, and we saw this man. My dad recognized him, went to him, and said, "How are you doing? Tudor's in town, and he's preaching for us…" He said to my dad, "I'm dying of cancer." That was something totally different than what he previously had, but there was no grace to pray for him that day.

So, the gift of faith is not like anointing. The gift of faith is the ability to believe to the point where it is impossible to have unbelief. It's impossible to entertain anything but great faith.

I experienced this gift during a meeting in Cayman Islands in 1993. It's as if the gift of faith came into that building one night when there were 2,000 people in attendance. There were over 2,000 miracles that took place because people were getting multiple miracles within days.

I recall a forum where Oral Roberts was sharing with a group of us at a roundtable discussion. Reverend Roberts had tent crusades for many years where so many thousands of people were healed all over the world. He said in some of his services they'd have him sit in a chair so people could pass by, and he could pray for them. The anointing was so strong and people were pulling so much that he couldn't stand. I asked Reverend Roberts a question: "Tell us about that open heaven you had." He said that at a service in one of his tent crusades, just before he got up to speak one night, something came into the room; everything within a radius of, I don't know how many miles—anybody that was in the crusade, not in the crusade, that wanted to be healed, didn't want to be healed—everyone in that radius got healed. It was the gift of faith—the gift of faith! When you have that kind of anointing, when you have the gift of faith, it's the currency of the Kingdom.

Let's look more closely at the three uses of the word "faith" we discussed earlier:

a) The faith that "pleases God" is faith that you grow. Romans 12:3 says, "… think soberly, according as God hath dealt to every man the measure of faith." It says every man has been given **the** measure of faith. **The** measure of faith is the ability to believe. That's what it means: the ability to believe. Every person has the ability to believe. You see it from the time a baby is small, and the dad says, "Jump, jump!" The baby believes in her dad because the baby has **the** measure, the ability to believe. Now how do you increase that? It comes by hearing; and hearing comes by the *rhema* word.

But here's the problem with this. James said in James 1:22, "Be ye doers of the Word, and not hearers only…" The way we hear determines how we do things because we all hear differently. Now listen to this: Every human being has a brain. Every brain has a mind. Every mind has a belief system or attitude. Every belief system or an attitude has a shaper; and every shaper has an agenda.

Everybody in the room can hear me, but not everybody hears me the same. When we hear a word, we are hearing on different levels. For some person, it's *rhema*; for some other person, it's not. For some person, it irritates; for some person, it's a blessing. The sun melts wax and hardens clay at the same time. The sun shines the same on both objects, but the outcome depends on their material.

So then, we have to train ourselves to hear. That's why there has to be a repetition of Scriptures to grow that measure of faith—to grow it, to grow it, to grow it. The Bible says, concerning this kind of faith, "the righteousness of God revealed from faith to faith." The way you get to the next level of faith is by your application of the Word—how you take it in and how you apply it. As you get the Word, you become a doer. Once you do it, you go to the next level. You have to grow your faith.

There are many, many writers who have written on faith: Charles Capps, E.W. Kenyon, Kenneth Hagin, Kenneth Copeland, Creflo Dollar, and Dr. Fred Price. All of them have written some of the most priceless books on faith. There are many others that have taught on the various aspects of faith. Reading books by men such as these is one way to grow your faith.

Another way to increase your faith is to actually ask God. In Luke 17:4, the disciples said, "Lord, increase our faith...." In another instance, when Jesus was asked to heal a child, He told the father that anything was possible if he could believe. Mark 9:24 then says, "And straightway the father of the child cried out, and said with tears, Lord, I believe; help thou mine unbelief." God hears us when we cry out to him. Ask Him for increase in your faith.

b) Fundamental faith relates to our doctrine. We must make sure that we know and understand our fundamental beliefs. One of the things we're going to do with our leadership is to study the Westminster Confession. A group of responsible leaders got together to write this confession to tackle the heresy that crept into the church in the 18th and 19th centuries. They came up with a framework of how we interpret Scriptures and how we come up with fundamental doctrine. Many evangelical groups have taken teachings and compromised them somewhat. It's important we have the fundamental beliefs with a foundation in the Word of God to build our faith upon.

c) The gift of faith comes in several ways. The first one is:
  1) We have to desire a spiritual gift. 1 Cor. 12:31 says, "But covet earnestly the best gifts."

  2) We have to be educated in spiritual gifts. Paul said in 1 Corinthians 12:1, "I would not that you be ignorant concerning spiritual gifts." We must be aware of how these gifts function and what they are.

  3) Matthew 17:21—The disciples tried unsuccessfully to cast a demon out of a man. Jesus told them the reason

they were unsuccessful was due to their unbelief. He said, "This kind comes out by prayer and fasting." There must be prayer and fasting to release faith at this level. So, first, we have to desire it. Second, we have to be educated in it. Third, we have to fast and pray. Now for the final way to increase faith:

4) We must keep on talking about it, because that's activation. When we talk about the gift of faith, we begin to expect it. We profess faith, we confess faith. The more it is spoken with the mouth, the more it infiltrates the mind and encourages the spirit. Talk about your faith all the time, giving testimonies and glory to God. Stir up the gifts in you, and release faith into the atmosphere around you. Recall the man we just spoke of in Mark 9:24 who said, "I believe, help my unbelief!" When God comes into the room, He believes for you because you can't believe for yourself. Another example to support this thought is from John 5:5–8:

> *And a certain man was there, which had an infirmity thirty and eight years. When Jesus saw him lie, and knew that he had been now a long time in that case, he saith unto him, Wilt thou be made whole? The impotent man answered him, Sir, I have no man, when the water is troubled, to put me into the pool: but while I am coming, another steppeth down before me. Jesus saith unto him, Rise, take up thy bed, and walk.*

This man was there for 38 years. He could not believe. Jesus believed for him. In a lot of places, Jesus saw faith in people and said to them, "Your faith has made you whole." But in some cases, He believed for them.

Sometimes we just want the easy way. We just want the gift of faith to come in and heal so that it goes outside of our belief, outside of our ability to believe. We want God to believe on our behalf because we cannot believe.

Now I can believe for you. I have in my own ministry life. I don't want to say or confess something in a negative way, but I think it's okay within the context of what I'm trying to say in this particular place. My major gift is not praying for the sick to be healed. I've prayed for many people, and they've been healed; but that's not my major gift. If you come to our church on a Sunday, I'm not going to be calling for the sick to pray for them. But I do have a gift in specific lines of healing:

1. In my lifetime of teaching, I think there are over 600 women that we have prayed for who could not have children that have children now. I have a gift to pray against barrenness.

Some years ago, on a Sunday morning, I was preaching at the International Conference Center, and I called a doctor forward along with his wife. I said, "You are going to have a son; his name will be Michael, and he's going to be a sign of your medical business that's coming as a breakthrough." Well, the previous Friday, she had been told for the 8th time, "You'll never have children." She was a dentist; he was a doctor. They recorded the prophetic word I told them that day, and they played that prophecy every day. They came to visit me several months later, and she was expecting a baby. She had just had a scan that day and the doctor told her, "You are having a son." So they came to show me that Michael was on the way. It's my gift, and I can tell you story after story.

I was preaching for Bishop Eddie Long many years ago. I remember it was a Monday night. Earlier that day, I'd eaten some salmon, and it gave me food poisoning. In the middle of my message, while I was preaching, I collapsed behind the pulpit. They had to carry me out of the meeting and take me to the hospital. The doctor who took me to the hospital that night was Dr. Harper, a member of that church. He took me to a trauma center and, of course, they did all kinds of stuff: I.V.'s, blood tests, and so on. Bishop Long came about midnight after they had settled the congregation, and they discharged me about two o'clock in the morning.

I was so grateful. Dr. Harper covered all the costs I had incurred. Anyway, long story short, Dr. Harper said, "Just pray for me because my wife and I have been married for 14 years; and we've just not been able to have children." So I prayed for them right there in the hospital room and left.

A year later, I was back at Bishop Eddie Long's doing the same January meetings for him. They were doing a baby dedication that morning, and he asked me to come join him because part of the dedication was Dr. Harper and his wife and their twin girls. So I prayed with them, and I said, "Next time, you're going to have a son." And so, they've had a son since that time.

I was in New Zealand last year, and there was a couple in a church working with the sound and worship team. They'd been married for 15 years or so and couldn't have children. Because they are Samoans, the wife must have children or else—you know, it's like in Africa. We prayed for them. I got a phone call from that church recently, and one of the things they told me is that this couple is having a baby. That baby will be born in May, and they are hoping that when we visit New Zealand, we will be able to dedicate that baby—after 15 years. It's just one of my giftings.

2. One of my other giftings is healing of hearts and ears. I have prayed for many people who have ear problems, and they've been healed.

There are times and places when I've seen the gift of faith come in a place. I was in Honduras and there was a preacher from Guatemala that was there with us. His name was Pastor Cash Luna. My assignment was to preach a prosperity message, and he was invited because he has the gift of miracles.

At the end of my message, people starting rushing the altar with money, just rushing the altar; the gift of faith came into that place. That building would seat 15,000, but there must have been 25,000 people there. The gift of faith came in there because when Pastor Cash Luna started to pray, there were all kinds of miracles.

There was a child who looked like his kidney was growing outside his body. The mother was showing Pastor Cash Luna how that kidney was improperly formed outside his body—and it just sucked into his body—it was incredible! I've got some video footage on my phone of three people that came out of wheelchairs that day. The authorities there verified the miracles were authentic.

Every now and then, the gift of faith comes into the environment. In the Cayman Islands one night, when the power of God hit that place, there were miracles that were taking place that lasted through the afterglow of that gift of faith. The afterglow lasted six weeks. Sometimes when the gift of faith comes in a place, boom! The afterglow is like concentric circles when you throw a stone in a pond. The afterglow can sometimes last for weeks. That's the gift of faith.

Now there's one final thing on faith that I want to mention. 1 Corinthians 13:13 says, "Now abideth faith, hope, and charity…" It's abiding faith. It's the Word of God that upholds everything by the word of His power. According to Hebrews 11:3, it's "By faith we understand that the worlds were framed by the word of God, so that the things which are seen were not made of things which are visible." By faith we understand that the worlds were framed by the word of God. Hebrews 1:3—"He is the radiance of the glory of God and the exact imprint of his nature, and he upholds the universe by the word of his power." By the word of His power, He upholds all things. It's called abiding faith. Everything in the molecular world is joined together by abiding faith. Even people who do not believe in God, and they do not believe in Jesus, live within the realm of abiding faith. Every human being believes on some level.

A person that's a God-hater who is going to marry someone may not believe in God, but they believe that the person they are marrying loves them. They don't believe in God; they hate Jesus, but they believe that the boss they've worked with for 30 days is going to pay them. They don't believe in God, but they believe that the bus they get into is going to take them to their destination. That's called abiding faith.

Unity

The strength of the Kingdom is unity, agreement. Matthew 18:19 says, "Again I say unto you, That if two of you shall agree on earth as touching anything that they shall ask, it shall be done for them of my Father which is in heaven." In the human realm, if we agree for a "thing," it shall be done. That's the strength of the Kingdom. All you need is one person to agree with you. Let me show you something that's important. If you have somebody that's a friend, whether it's a husband or a wife, or a colleague, who starts saying something stupid or wallowing in self-pity, tell them, "I do not agree with you." You must tell them right there, "I do not agree with you." If you agree with them, it shall be done.

One time a guy told me, "All you preachers do is preach money, and the next thing that happens is that money is going to be coming into your church in wheelbarrows." I said, "I agree with you!" If I had defended myself and said, "I don't agree with you," then I would be limiting the fact because somebody here will come with a wheelbarrow load of money just to prove it. Are we together? You need to find somebody that can agree with you.

The Bible says in Genesis 11:6 that "...Behold, the people is one, and they have all one language; and this they begin to do: and now nothing will be restrained from them, which they have imagined to do." In Psalm 133:1,3, we see, "Behold, how good and how pleasant it is for brethren to dwell together in unity! ...for there the Lord commanded the blessing, even life for evermore."

When men and brethren dwell together in unity, the Bible says that it is good and it's pleasant because there God commands THE blessing. God commands THE blessing, even life forevermore. So in agreement, there's power.

ChiChi and I have noticed that when a couple is about to come into a breakthrough either as a couple or as a family, suddenly contention arises in their home, and sometimes even in ours. Arguments ensue, taking the couple to a place of dis-agreement. The word, disagreement is two words; dis- and agreement, which means your agreement has been dissed. The minute the agreement is dissed, unity is gone, and the power of agreement is broken. There's strength and power in agreement; we must commit to unity and fight for agreement. The strength of the Kingdom is unity.

CHAPTER 10
UNDERSTANDING MYSTERIES

The access to the Kingdom comes through understanding mysteries. The key Scripture we will reference is in Matthew 13:10–12:

> *And the disciples came, and said unto him, Why speakest thou unto them in parables? He answered and said unto them, Because it is given unto you to know the mysteries of the kingdom of heaven, but to them it is not given. For whosoever hath, to him shall be given, and he shall have more abundance: but whosoever hath not, from him shall be taken away even that he hath. Therefore speak I to them in parables: because they seeing see not; and hearing they hear not, neither do they understand."*

The disciples asked Jesus this question just after He had completed the parable of the sower and the seed. Jesus told them, "It is given unto you to know the mysteries of the Kingdom of Heaven, but to them, it is not given.'" It's given to you; it is not given to them. So understanding mysteries then is something that is given. There are people to whom understanding mysteries is given, and to some it is not given. From our study, I will show you that you, too, can understand mysteries. We need to ask the Lord to give us understanding of mysteries because, when we understand mysteries, we have access to the Kingdom.

Now look at the backdrop of this revelation; it is between parables that Jesus is explaining this dynamic. He continues to explain, telling them that if you have understanding, more will be given; if you don't, even what you have will be taken away. He speaks to the people in parables, which is simply a heavenly story with an earthly meaning. The word parable also means pictures or word pictures.

Jesus said the reason He speaks to them in heavenly stories with earthly meanings or in pictures is because they do not understand mysteries. To you it is given; to them it is not—to you it is given. So what are pictures, then? A picture is given to those that are not mature. A picture is for babies.

In kindergarten, the teacher uses pictures to teach the students letters and sounds. She'll say, "A" is for apple. When the children see the apple, they associate the picture of the apple with the picture of the letter "A". Likewise, "B" is for ball or banana; "C" is for cat; "D" is for dog. This progression continues through the alphabet, showing the children pictures in order to teach them the letter. Messages presented with many stories are usually given to immature people, those unable to grasp the strong meat of the Word. Picture preaching doesn't build strong believers. In this passage, Jesus basically said, "You do not need picture preaching; you understand mysteries. To others, I talk in pictures because they don't understand mysteries."

I want you to look very closely now at Matthew 13:15:

> *For this people's heart is waxed gross, and their ears are dull of hearing, and their eyes they have closed; lest at any time they should see with their eyes and hear with their ears, and should understand with their heart, and should be converted, and I should heal them. But blessed are your eyes, for they see: and your ears, for they hear.*

The passage says, "this people's heart has waxed gross," meaning their hearts had become fat and dull. They had become dull at hearing; overweight. Their ears had become heavy and difficult of hearing. Their eyes were tightly closed. Watch this important process:

Mysteries are revealed through the following progression:

1. You see with your eyes.
2. You hear with your ears.
3. You grasp with your heart.

Then healing comes; it's right there. Understand mysteries: see with your eyes; hear with your ears; understand with your heart; healing comes. When you have a group of people or a generation that cannot access mysteries, they must be trained to see with their eyes, hear with their ears, and understand with their hearts; then healing comes. When Jesus brought the apostles into His domain, into His ministry, He had to do three things with them.

1. He had to open their eyes to see.
2. He had to open their ears to hear.
3. He had to open their hearts to receive.

By the time they got to the events in Matthew 13, that progression had taken place in their lives. Now look at Matthew 10, and let's see how Jesus was doing this with the apostles. Matthew 10:1: "And when he had called unto him his twelve disciples, he gave them power against unclean spirits, to cast them out, and to heal all manner of sickness and all manner of disease." Let's continue with verses 5 through 7 with what I call the Apostles Manual: "These twelve Jesus sent forth, and commanded them, saying, Go not into the way of the Gentiles, and into any city of the Samaritans enter ye not: But go rather to the lost sheep of the house of Israel. And as ye go, preach, saying, The kingdom of heaven is at hand."

Look what He says—"Do not go to the Gentiles; do not go into any of the cities of the Samaritans; don't even enter there. Go to the lost sheep of the house of Israel. As you go, preach, saying, 'The Kingdom of Heaven has landed; The Kingdom of Heaven is manifested.'" He's giving them power over sickness and disease; He tells them to go, although, at this point, they don't even know who they are.

He sent them forth two-by-two. He told them to preach the Kingdom, heal the sick, cleanse the lepers, raise the dead, and cast out devils, because freely you've received, so freely give. He goes on to tell them the many things that will manifest in their lives. The first way that Jesus is going to help them see mysteries is to open their eyes. They have to see who they are; they have to see the power they've been given. Next, they have to hear His word; they have to hear. He said, "Preach the Kingdom." So once they've seen what they've seen and heard what they've heard, their hearts became converted. They became conditioned to receive the word or the message of the Kingdom.

By the time they got to the events in Matthew 13, their eyes were opened to see; their ears were opened to hear; and their hearts had been opened to receive. Jesus said, 'the difference between you and these people— you were where these people are; your eyes couldn't see; your ears couldn't hear; your heart couldn't receive. Now your eyes see, "Blessed are your eyes for they see; blessed are your ears for they hear…" and your heart is opened. So the way we receive mysteries, the way we access the Kingdom is to get people conditioned where their eyes can see, ears can hear, and their hearts can receive.

Let me show you how this works based on Adam. Let's go to Genesis 3:1 and look at some interesting terminology: "Now the serpent was more subtle than any beast of the field which the LORD God had made. And he said unto the woman, Yea, hath God said, Ye shall not eat of every tree of the garden?" The serpent was more subtle or crafty than any of the creatures of the field that the LORD God had made." So satan then used the serpent to speak to the woman. The woman said to the serpent in verses 2 and 3:"We may eat of the fruit of the trees of the garden. But of the fruit of the tree which is in the midst of the garden, God hath said, Ye shall not eat of it, neither shall ye touch it, lest ye die."

Watch this very carefully. God had spoken to Adam long before Eve was in the garden and said to Adam in Genesis 2:16,17: "And the LORD God commanded the man, saying, Of every tree of the garden thou mayest freely eat: But of the tree of the knowledge of good and evil, thou shalt not eat of it: for in the day that thou eatest thereof thou shalt surely die." God told Adam, "You're not to eat that fruit." When Eve came along, she said exactly what God had told Adam. God never told Eve, "Don't eat of that fruit." He never told her that; God told Adam. So who told Eve? Adam told Eve. Adam was a good teacher because God never said to Eve personally, "Don't eat of that; and don't touch it."

When Eve came out of Adam's side in Genesis 2:23, he said "...this is woman; this is bone of my bone and flesh of my flesh." Adam then, in the realm of awareness, told his wife everything that God had told him. Adam was the apostle. The apostle got his word from God. The apostle told his wife and opened her eyes and ears to truth and her heart to receive truth. Therefore, she understood the mysteries in the garden.

When the serpent, the devil, spoke to Eve, she rehearsed the mysteries of the Kingdom to the devil. Now watch what the devil does in Genesis 3:4; it's demonic strategy. "And the serpent said to the woman, you shall not surely die." So he sowed an idea of something into her heart that was not previously there.

She had not experienced death; they didn't know what death was. They had no point of reference as to what death was from any references in the Scriptures. The Bible doesn't say that animals died; we're not sure that they did. We're not sure that there was any form of death there. There may have been a point of reference where animals had died, but even so, Adam and Eve were in a place where they could not die.

Watch this in verse 5: The devil said, "For God doth know that in the day ye eat thereof, then your eyes shall be opened, and ye shall be as gods, knowing good and evil." Was Eve blind? No, she was not blind. So what did the devil mean, "...your eyes shall be opened." He's dealing with a principle as to how mysteries function. Now watch, when he gave her that fact, look what happened in verse 6: "The woman saw that the tree was good for food and that it was pleasant to the eyes...."

She'd been looking at that thing for a while; I don't know how many years, decades, or even centuries; we don't know. Now that the idea was introduced to her, even though she was not blind, she saw. The way mysteries open is our responsibility. Jesus said that the first step to helping people understand mysteries is to teach them in parables so they see a word picture. It's just like giving babies milk that they can easily eat and digest before giving them meat. Begin with something simpler to help them develop before graduating to the heavier material.

Look with me at 2 Thessalonians 2:7: "For the mystery of lawlessness (that hidden principle of rebellion against constituted authority) is already at work in the world, [but it is] restrained only until he who restrains is taken out of the way" (AMP). Here the Apostle Paul mentions something that is very interesting: "For the mystery of iniquity does already work." The mystery of iniquity, the mystery of lawlessness, or the mystery of the principles of rebellion against authority is already at work in the world. So the mystery of iniquity was already in existence when Eve was in the garden with Adam. The mystery of iniquity, the mystery of rebellion against God was already there. But she couldn't see it. So the devil had to open her eyes.

When he opened her eyes, suddenly, now she could see and now she could hear, and her heart had become conditioned for the fruit on the tree to be sown in her heart. When she did that, she activated something that was already at work within her that she couldn't see. So around me, around you, there are mysteries that are in existence, but they cannot be activated until we see and hear and our hearts are conditioned.

When we understand mysteries, we have access to the Kingdom. Go now to Ephesians 3:3—the Apostle Paul says,

> *If ye have heard of the dispensation of the grace of God*
> *which is given me to you-ward: How that by revelation*
> *he made known unto me the mystery; (as I wrote afore in*
> *few words, whereby, when ye read, ye may understand my*

knowledge in the mystery of Christ) Which in other ages
was not made known unto the sons of men, as it is now
revealed unto his holy apostles and prophets by the Spirit.

Let's break that down just a little. Paul said that, by revelation, I've been given the grace to understand mysteries. He says, in times past, the sons of men couldn't understand it. Why? Because when Adam and Eve sinned against God, their eyes closed. Their spiritual eyes closed. They couldn't see. Their spiritual ears closed. They couldn't hear. Their heart became hardened. They couldn't get saved. They couldn't. So for decades, for centuries, people couldn't understand or even experience revelation knowledge with the mysteries of the Kingdom.

The first one really to begin to break that down started with Noah. He got a bit of an insight. Then came Abraham,...Isaac,...Jacob,...Joseph, and then slavery. When Moses came, he brought liberation to three and a half million people for a simple reason. Moses' eyes were opened. When Moses saw the fire in the burning bush, his eyes were opened. Moses' ears were opened; then his heart was converted. After that happened, Moses was able to deliver, in a short space of time, people who had been enslaved for over 400 years. Take a moment to say, "My eyes are opened; my ears can hear; my heart is conditioned...for the Kingdom to be planted."

The Bible says in Ephesians 3:5: "It is now revealed unto His holy apostles and prophets by the Spirit." So mysteries are understood by apostles and prophets. So what makes an apostle? Definitely, it's somebody that does not work in pictures. My responsibility for people that cannot hear, cannot see, and cannot understand is to paint the picture for you, but I don't work in pictures. When God speaks to me, He has to speak to me in lateral and vertical truths that can be translated to make them applicable to our surroundings.

Please watch now as I come to the conclusion of this presentation on mysteries. In the teaching of mysteries, there are many things we can say and many differences of opinions regarding mysteries, depending on your teacher. There are fourteen different named mysteries in the Bible; however, I prefer to put them in the category of seven mysteries because seven seems easier to work with.

Let me give you examples of several of the named mysteries.

a) 2 Timothy 3:16 reads, "And without controversy great is the mystery of godliness: God was manifest in the flesh, justified in the Spirit, seen of angels, preached unto the Gentiles, believed on in the world, received up into glory."

b) Ephesians 5:24–25,28 refers to the mystery of Christ and the church: " Husbands, love your wives, even as Christ also loved the church, and gave himself for it; That he might sanctify and cleanse it with the washing of water by the word," V. 28: "This is a great mystery: but I speak concerning Christ and the church.

c) 2 Thessalonians 2:7 is the mystery of iniquity, "For the mystery of iniquity doth already work: only he who now letteth will let, until he be taken out of the way."

d) 1 Corinthians 15:51 reveals the mystery of the translation of the saints. "Behold, I shew you a mystery; We shall not all sleep, but we shall all be changed, In a moment, in the twinkling of an eye, at the last trump: for the trumpet shall sound, and the dead shall be raised incorruptible, and we shall be changed"

Although there are many of these mysteries, the mystery of the Kingdom is what we want to investigate. The mystery of the Kingdom includes the character and the actions of God within the earth. The word 'mystery' comes from the Greek word, *musterion*, which actually means 'message in a code' or a coded message. So for you to access the mystery, you need to understand the code. For you to understand the code, you need to understand the language. So the Kingdom of God has a language.

So what's the language of the Kingdom of God? Let's go to 1 Corinthians 14:2–5:

> *For he that speaketh in an unknown tongue speaketh*
> *not unto men, but unto God: for no man understandeth*
> *him; howbeit in the spirit he speaketh mysteries." But*
> *he that prophesieth speaketh unto men to edification,*
> *and exhortation, and comfort. He that speaketh in an*
> *unknown tongue edifieth himself; but he that prophesieth*
> *edifieth the church. I would that ye all spake with tongues*
> *but rather that ye prophesied: for greater is he that*
> *prophesieth than he that speaketh with tongues, except he*
> *interpret, that the church may receive edifying.*

Some of the greatest churches I've been to in the world are churches that spend a lot of time praying in the Spirit. When you have churches or people like that, preachers who visit there preach stronger than anywhere else they've been. One of the reasons is that the church that spends a lot of time praying is bringing mysteries low. When you pray in an unknown tongue, you are speaking mysteries. You are bringing mysteries so low that they will be easy to enter into. Mysteries are revealed through two things: **First**, pray in the Spirit to break codes. When you pray in the Spirit, there are four things happening in you:

a) When you pray in the Spirit, you are edifying and building up yourself.

b) When you pray in the Spirit you are praying mysteries. As you pray mysteries in the Spirit—God will give you the code to decode the mystery.

c) When you pray in the Spirit, it actually means you speak the languages of different places. In Mark 16:17, Jesus says, "And these signs will accompany those who believe: In my name they will drive out demons; they will speak in new tongues...."

Speaking in tongues there actually means the languages of different places.

d) When you pray in the Spirit, your tongue can address national or global events on a national level. Isaiah 28:11,12 says, "For with stammering lips and another tongue will he speak to this people. To whom he said, This is the rest wherewith ye may cause the weary to rest; and this is the refreshing: yet they would not hear." So your tongue can address national or global events on a national level.

The more you speak in tongues, the more access you can have to the mysteries of heaven. Paul said, "I thank God I speak in tongues more than you all," in 1 Corinthians 14:18. That's one of the reasons he had so many revelations because he spent much of his life speaking in tongues. You don't have to be in a prayer meeting to pray in the Spirit. You can pray in the Spirit in the shower, cooking food, ironing clothes…..wherever you are, you can pray in the Spirit.

Second, mysteries are revealed through the Word. Read this verse from Romans 16: 25,26. "Now to him that is of power to stablish you according to my gospel and the preaching of Jesus Christ according to the revelation of the mystery which was kept secret since the world began, but now is made manifest and by the scriptures of the prophets… made known to all the nations…"

So, first, mysteries are uncovered when you understand codes and break them by the Spirit. The second way mysteries are uncovered is by the Scriptures.

You must spend time in the Scriptures because it's the living Word of God. Read with me in Luke 24:45—"Then He opened their understanding to understand the Scriptures." The amazing thing about that verse is that Jesus is speaking to these individuals who had been with Him for three and a half years. They'd heard Him teach. They'd seen Him perform every conceivable miracle, but even after three and a half years, they still needed to have their understanding opened to the Scriptures. Put your hand on your head and say, "Open my understanding to understand the Scriptures."

I'll list two ways below to help you understand the Scriptures:

1. The first way is to spend time in it; read and study the Word. "Study to show yourself approved unto God a workman that needeth not to be ashamed rightly dividing the Word of God." 2 Timothy 2:15. You have to rightly divide. That means line upon line, metaphor on metaphor will help you understand the mysteries. Say, "I understand mysteries." Say it again. Say it one more time.

2. The second way to understand Scripture is by prophetic utterance. You have to learn the powers of prophetic utterance. We have to understand how prophetic utterance works because it can be a pretty amazing thing. Read with me in Colossians 1:26. "Even the mystery which has been hidden from ages and from generations but is now made manifest to His saints." It's now made manifest. So it's God's will for me to understand mysteries. It was hidden in other ages; it was hidden in other generations; but it is now made manifest to His saints to whom God would make known what is the riches of the glory of this mystery among the Gentiles. My question is: Are you a Gentile? You are a Gentile; you're not a Jew; you are a Gentile.

We will look at one last passage here in the Book of Daniel, Chapter 1, verses 19 and 20:

And the king communed with them; and among them all
was found none like Daniel, Hananiah, Mishael, and
Azariah: therefore stood they before the king. And in

all matters of wisdom and understanding, that the king
enquired of them, he found them ten times better than all
the magicians and astrologers that were in all his realm.

In all matters of wisdom, in all matters of understanding that the king inquired of them, these boys were ten times better. Ten times better than whom? All the magicians, all the astrologers, and all that were in his realm. Look at verse 17: "For these four, God gave them knowledge and skill in all learning and wisdom; and Daniel had understanding in all visions and dreams." They were accessing mysteries to get into the Kingdom. Go back to verse 20. In all these things God made them ten times better than ALL the wise men. Put your hand on your head and say, "I understand mysteries; therefore, I am ten times better." I am convinced that we are going to have a generation that will unleash a thousand years of the Kingdom in the earth that is right here, reading this book. Something's going to jump on you that's going to make you ten times better than all. And when we are ten times better, we will begin to displace the influence, the knowledge and the power of the devil. There are people to whom it is not given; but to me it is given. My eyes see; my ears hear; my heart is open; and I am healed.

God has given us the power to understand mysteries. It is God's will. When we pray, we pray, "Thy will be done on earth as it is in heaven." What is God's will? His will for me is to understand mysteries. When I understand mysteries, I have access to the Kingdom of God.

CHAPTER 11

REVELATION KNOWLEDGE

As we consider the dynamics of the Kingdom and realize that access to the Kingdom comes through understanding mysteries, we desire more revelation knowledge.

Revelation knowledge is going to come in one of four ways:

1. The first way revelation knowledge comes is by schooling. You go to school, and you learn the basic or fundamental principles which are the basis for all your knowledge in the years to come. You enter in at the basic principle level. Once you master the basic principle level, it then depends on how far YOU want to go. If you want to do math, you can do algebra, geometry, calculus, Pythagoras—whatever the situation might be, it just depends on how far you want to go.

Take the Swiss inventors, for instance. They've invented hovercrafts that work with micro sensors and laser beam sensors that can pick up an object, then fly and do almost anything; it's the transportation of the future. There'll be no fuel; it's all done by computers; The guy that was working out the mathematical formula was showing the guy from CNN how this thing works—it was $XZM^2 = YZ$. After he was writing XZ plus something, he lost me because I've been struggling with my math from numbers 0 to 9. These guys entered at the basic level and didn't stop—they kept going and are still going.

All music is built on seven notes. There are over 5,000 songs written every day in the world, all based on seven notes. It depends on how far you want to go whether you're going to write a piece like Tchaikovsky or Mendelsohn or Beethoven or Mozart; it just depends on how far you want to go.

The same is true with language. In our language, it's just 26 letters of the alphabet on frames of two- and three-letter words that form small little sentences based on phonetics. And then it just depends, in the world of language, on how far you want to go.

Revelation comes from education. We should never stop being students.

2. The second way revelation comes is the Greek word "gnosis". Gnosis means experiences that produce knowledge. Therefore, the older person will teach the younger.

That's what Paul told Titus in Titus 2:3–5. He said:

> *Older women likewise are to be reverent in behavior,*
> *not slanderers or slaves to much wine. They are*
> *to teach what is good, and so train the young*
> *women to love their husbands and children, to be*
> *self-controlled, pure, working at home, kind, and*
> *submissive to their own husbands, that the word of*
> *God may not be reviled.*

In other words, life will teach you lessons. Some of the wisest people I know never went to school. One of them was Bishop Kasese, whose children and grandchildren serve in the church.

There was another man that I used to work with who counseled with me. He was at our conference although I'd not seen him in many, many years, and now he's about 89 years old. His name was Brother Chilonga, and he never went to school. He was from Malawi and many times walked a route from Harare to Salisbury. He would tell me that, on that route, there were certain places with trees that had ropes. At night, people who were walking that route would climb those trees and tie themselves in with the ropes because of the lions. Brother Chilonga never went to school, but some of the most incredible counsel, wisdom and knowledge that I ever got from anybody came from those men that never went to school.

That's revelation through life. If life hasn't taught you any lessons, you have a foolish, unteachable spirit! You should not be repeating the same mistakes over and over and over again. Life should have taught you something. That's why, when you go through a test or a trial, it's an honor and a privilege because you are about to discover a truth that you cannot find in a book. There are lessons that can only be learned through a life experience.

If you've never had a baby, you cannot tell someone what it feels like. You read it in a book and if you are a midwife, you can say the dilations are like this; the contractions are like this; but until you are in the position and you are saying, **"JESUS,"** you'll never really be able to relate. It becomes a privilege when you go through something.

3. The third way Revelation knowledge comes is through what the Hebrews call YADA or Y-A-D-A-H. That's revelation knowledge that comes when heaven opens. Matthew 16:13–17 ESV is a prime example of revelation knowledge from heaven:

Now when Jesus came into the district of Caesarea Philippi, he asked his disciples, "Who do people say that the Son of Man is?" And they said, "Some say John the Baptist, others say Elijah, and others Jeremiah or one of the prophets." He said to them,

"But who do you say that I am?" Simon Peter replied, "You are the Christ, the Son of the living God." And Jesus answered him, "Blessed are you, Simon Bar-Jonah! For flesh and blood has not revealed this to you, but my Father who is in heaven." (ESV).

Simon Peter's response to Jesus' question was, "You are the Christ, the Son of the Living God." Jesus said, "Peter, flesh and blood [that's revelation by schooling] has not revealed this to you. This is from my Father which is in heaven." This is revelation from heaven, YADA. This kind of revelation comes when your eyes see, your ears hear, and your heart is in condition. Put your right hand on your head and say, "Give me revelation."

In John 3:2–5, Nicodemus came to Jesus with questions:

The same came to Jesus by night, and said unto him, Rabbi, we know that thou art a teacher come from God: for no man can do these miracles that thou doest, except God be with him. Jesus answered and said unto him, Verily, verily, I say unto thee, Except a man be born again, he cannot see the kingdom of God. Nicodemus saith unto him, How can a man be born when he is old? can he enter the second time into his mother's womb, and be born? Jesus answered, Verily, verily, I say unto thee, Except a man be born of water and of the Spirit, he cannot enter into the kingdom of God.

If you want to see it, if you want to enter into it, you have to be born again. "Verily, verily, I say unto you except a man be born again, he cannot see…" Being born again means a change of mind, a conditioning of the heart, so for you to enter into the mystery of the Kingdom, you have to have your mind changed; your eyes have to see.

In Ephesians 1:9, Paul says, "Having made known unto us the mystery of his will, according to his good pleasure which he hath purposed in himself." God has made known the mystery of His will. How is the mystery revealed: eyes see; ears hear; a heart is conditioned.

Go on to Ephesians 1:16 and see what Paul says to the Ephesian church now that eyes are opened, ears hear, and hearts are conditioned: "I do not cease giving thanks for you, making mention of you in my prayers..." Now this is what he prayed: "That the God of our Lord Jesus Christ, the Father of glory, may give unto you the spirit of wisdom and revelation in the knowledge of him: The eyes of your understanding being enlightened..."

In your Bible, underline or highlight this: "The eyes of your understanding being enlightened..." The way a mystery lands in your life is that the eyes of your understanding open. Stop a moment and ask the Lord, "Open my eyes." When your eyes open, you condition yourself for a YADA moment, a revelation that flesh and blood cannot reveal to you.

It's good to go to Bible School; you receive revelation through schooling because you're going to learn basic, fundamental principles for ministry. School teaches us the *logos* word and the practical application of it. You need to get to a place, into a position where you get the *rhema* word where heaven opens and God gives you a revelation.

4. The fourth way revelation comes is the word SOD. This is where revelation knowledge comes in a cluster or a company. The Bibles says in 1 Samuel 10, when Samuel pours the oil on Saul, he says, there are three signs coming. First, you'll go to Rachel's sepulcher; they'll tell you that the donkeys are found. Second, you'll meet three men, one carrying three loaves of bread, one carrying goat meat on his head, and another carrying a bottle

of wine. He said, thirdly, you're going to get to Bethel and find a company of prophets coming down from Bethel. When you come to the company of prophets, you, Saul, will prophesy with them and you will become another man. That's a summary of verses 1–3 in 1 Samuel 10.

Now look at this very carefully. Samuel is one of the greatest prophets of all time. When Saul came into Samuel's presence, Samuel did not make that man prophesy. He didn't—even though he was one of the greatest prophets of all time. But when Saul came to Bethel, there was a company of prophets. All of those men were of lesser rank than Samuel, but the collective, corporate gifting and anointing of them collectively was greater than that of the one man who was greater than each of them. The company of prophets didn't force Saul to prophesy, the corporate anointing caused him to prophesy.

Anointing then comes when inspiration comes in a cluster. It's one idea that produces an idea. It's a revelation that is the anchor to birth more revelation. The anchor revelation, which is YADA, has to be the anchor for SOD because YADA opens the door for the cluster. Now let me put it to you in ordinary terms.

I met a man not so long ago in Zimbabwe. His family was living on almost one dollar a day; the generation before that was living on even less than that. His father was earning one shilling a week, the equivalent of ten cents. But his generation, about 15 years ago, was earning a dollar a day, one American dollar a day. That's thirty dollars a month. His family was living on thirty dollars a month.

Some sort of mineral wealth was discovered on their land, and a group came from South Africa with money in a briefcase. They had $200,000 in a briefcase and showed this man the money. And the family went wild when they saw $200,000. Remember what he was earning—his father was earning a shilling a week and he was earning a dollar a day. They had never seen so much money in their lives. They took the money, but the truth of the matter is that the company that came and offered him the money for the mineral wealth generated 2.5 billion dollars from that place in five years.

When you get a revelation, that's not where you stop. What they should have said is: "Two hundred thousand dollars is the entry fee for you to come on to this land. And then, for all of the mineral wealth that you get out of here, we are demanding not less than 10% of the proceeds." If they had done that, which is SOD, they would have walked out with two hundred and fifty million dollars, not $200,000!

This is representative of one of the problems with Africans. We get a car, and we think we have arrived. God wants you to own the car factory. That's SOD. YADA is the car. You get a new suit, and you think you look nice. God doesn't want you to just own a suit; He wants you to own the clothing factory. So, my point here in colloquial terms, painting with pictures, is that once you have a YADA moment, it becomes the step for a SOD experience. That means, you get the first one; that's the anchor. When you get a million dollars, it's the first of many millions. When you get a house, it's the first of many properties. When you get a child, it's the first of many children.

As our desire to enter into the fullness of the Kingdom grows, we long to operate within the ten Kingdom dynamics; our responsibility lies in seeking the Kingdom, seeking the knowledge, and seeking the revelation.

CONCLUSION
BE THE GENERATION

A generation will emerge that will not only preach the gospel of the Kingdom but also they will live it, testify and spread it. And when that generation comes, everything we see of satanic influence, everything we see as satanic behavior, everything we see as satanic, demonic strongholds will be displaced and will be cast down.

As we come to the end of this closing chapter, I want to remind you of the primary purpose of this book: to bring Increase to the Kingdom. Hopefully, throughout the messages taught here, seeds of understanding and enlightenment have been planted which will bring revelation to your patterns of thinking. Let me encourage you to water those seeds with the truth of the Word, sending those roots deep into good soil, building a solid structure bearing Kingdom fruit.

Now, please don't just read this book, and say, "Yeah, Bishop, this is good stuff." Be intentional; formulate a plan to bring increase to the Kingdom and teach others to do the same. Put your words into actions that will make a difference for yourself, your family, and your church, reaching even into the next generation.

Here's my challenge to you: Go back to the first section of this book and review the list of ten reasons we have problems and why problems arise. Identify the ones relevant to your life, if you haven't already done so, and attack them one by one. Remove or correct the issues you find, even if it requires a timely process. Correct foundational faults and errors, and start anew. Don't just make a difference—be the difference!

"With God, nothing is impossible."

Next, incorporate into your life the dynamics presented here to establish a Kingdom mindset which is essential to Kingdom living:

1. The nature of the Kingdom is increase.
2. The dynamics of the Kingdom is…everything gets better.
3. The power of the Kingdom is force.
4. The culture of the Kingdom is service.
5. The order of the Kingdom is structure.
6. The anointing of the Kingdom is gifts.
7. The success of the Kingdom is generational dominion.
8. The currency of the Kingdom is faith.
9. The strength of the Kingdom is unity.
10. The access to the Kingdom is understanding mysteries.

Lastly, unite and join forces with the church, which is the body of Christ. Stand with those who will displace the powers of darkness, by living, testifying, and spreading the gospel to bring Kingdom Increase. A generation is coming….and we can be that generation!

CONCLUSION: BE THE GENERATION

INCREASE OF THE KINGDOM

REFERENCES

http://humanprovincegreat.com

http://conflict.lshtm.ac.uk/page_05.htm#a_OUTLINE

Bailey, Alice (1972). *Serving Humanity.* Lucis Publishing Company.

Bailey, Alice (2011). *The Externalisation of the Hierarchy.* Lucis Publishing Company.

Bailey, Alice. "The 10 Point Plan by Alice Bailey for a New World Order" https://www.facebook.com/notes/pastor-david-ogbueli/the-10-point-plan-by-alice-bailey-and-the-new-world-order-for-the-destruction-of/10151669226247539

Bright, Bill. "Seven Mind Molders." http://unsettledchristianity.com/tag/bill-bright

Cunningham, Dr. Loren. "Seven Mountains" http://www.7culturalmountains.org

Guara, Deande. "7 Mind Molders" http://www.deandeguara.com

Munroe, Myles (2004). *Rediscovering the Kingdom.* Shippensburg, PA: Destiny Image Publishers.

Munroe, Myles (2006). *Kingdom Principles.* Shippensburg, PA: Destiny Image Publishers

Nye, Joseph (1991). *Bound to Lead: The Changing Nature of American Power*. Basic Books.

Pitts, Michael (2011). *Power Shifters*. Amazon Digital Services, Inc.

Varner, Kelley (2003). *Chosen for Greatness: Discover Your Personal Destiny*. Destiny Image Publishers.

Varner, Kelley (1998). *Corporate Anointing*. Destiny Image Publishers

Wallnau, Dr Lance. "Seven Mountains" http://unsettledchristianity. com/seven-mountains-Dr–Lance-Wallnau

Wallnau, Dr Lance. "Seven Mountain Strategy" http://lancewallnau.com